Jennie's Journal
by
Wyona Holmes Jaffe

Glorybound Publishing
Camp Verde, Arizona USA
in the year 2018

Jennie's Journal

2018 © Copyright Wyona Holmes Jaffe
Published by Glorybound Publishing, Camp Verde, AZ
SAN 256-4564
10 9 8 7 6 5 4 3 2 1
Printed in the United States of America
ISBN 978-1-60789-301-1 1-60789-301-0
KDP ISBN 9781080222124
Copyright data is available on file.
Jaffe, Wyona Holmes, 1937-
    Jennie's Journal
1. Historical Biography   2. Arizona History   I. Title

www.gloryboundpublishing.com

About the Cover

Tuzigoot National Monument located in Clarkdale, Arizona. This is the area where Jennie Lee was born. Photos by author. Insert photo of Jennie Lee Hawkins Holmes at age 11.

DEDICATION
This book is dedicated to my three children; Deborah Reeder, Mark Reeder, and Philip Reeder with the hope they will always be aware of their unique Arizona history.

Thanks

There are so many people involved, either directly or indirectly, with the writing of this book that I really don't know where to begin to pass out the "thanks." At the top of the list would have to be my daughter, Deborah, not only for being with me from the very beginning but for sticking with the project all the way through. She and I started the whole thing in 1977 by taping Grandma Jennie's oral history with the idea of eventually getting it down on paper. Deb was an invaluable help in the editing and the research.

I especially want to thank all of my many family members: husband Irv, parents, sisters, brothers, aunts, uncles, cousins, nephew, and distant relatives, who took the time to be interviewed, to help me do research, to answer my letters of inquiry, to loan me photos and irreplaceable keepsakes, and to otherwise have patience with me during the years I worked on this labor of love. I could not have done it without them.

The biggest "thank you" of all goes to the pioneers who had the courage to travel across the country to settle in this particular part of the world. They made it possible for me to live here and enjoy the perfect life I have to this day.

Endorsement

Wyona Jaffe, charter member of Beaver Creek Preservation and Historical Society, is a role model for us all when it comes to preserving history. She has spent many years recording her family's history which is so much a part of early pioneer life in the Verde Valley. The result of this research is <u>Jennie's Journal: 1875 True Story of a Verde Valley Pioneer.</u> Her personal high standards, tenacity and detailed research have resulted in this valuable resource and a legacy for all to enjoy. Thank you, Wyona.

Judy McBride,
President,
Beaver Creek Preservation and Historical Society
Retired Beaver Creek teacher and administrator

Letter from the Author

The story of the life of Jennie Lee Hawkins Holmes came about as a result of my interest in Arizona history in general and my family history in particular. My grandmother, Jennie Lee, was born in the Arizona Territory in February 1891. She passed on parts of the family history by telling the stories of her early life to her children and grandchildren. She also kept a personal journal, excerpts from which are to be found throughout this book.

To preserve these stories for future generations, my daughter Deborah and I began working with Grandma Jennie by putting her oral history on tapes. Little did we know what a big job it would turn out to be. One year from the day we started, Grandma died (on my birthday January 27, 1978), leaving us to continue to put the pieces together as best we could. We started by interviewing family members then progressed to doing research in libraries, courthouses, archives, historical societies, and museums. Ultimately, all this research required some major decisions about what to include and what to leave out from all the interesting information we had gathered. I published the first version in 1987 after moving to Lake Montezuma in the Verde Valley. During the ensuing 30 years I have lived here, I have come across many more stories about our family and their history. The revised version includes some of the other information I and other family members have discovered.

In keeping with our original idea of recording some interesting and informative facts about Grandma Jennie's life, this book is an attempt to give the reader a small glimpse into the life of a pioneer during the early days of Arizona. It is not intended to be a complete history, but all the information and anecdotes recorded are as factual as we were able to determine.

---Wyona Holmes Jaffe

Introduction

My story as a pioneer began in 1875 with a long, difficult journey from Missouri. My grandparents, William Henry, Sr. and Harriet Hawkins, along with ten of their thirteen children, traveled in a wagon train to the newly-settled Verde Valley in the Arizona Territory. My parents, William Henry, Jr., and Alice Smith Hawkins, followed them three years later with one-year-old Harriet (Hattie). They had nine more children while living in the Verde Valley, and I was born on February 26, 1891, the seventh of these ten children. In 1900 my mother died and my father took my two younger brothers Bill and Alvin, and sister Mary Alice and me to live with our married sister Hattie, in Phoenix. We eventually moved to Buckeye in 1904.

I married John Robert Holmes two years later, and we homesteaded in the vicinity of Buckeye and Cashion until we moved to Phoenix in 1923 when Robert was no longer able to do the heavy work on the ranch. Our five children grew up and finished their schooling in Phoenix. Robert and I had been married for 54 years when he died on November 11, 1962, shortly before his 82nd birthday.

This book is the true story of my life as told to my granddaughter, Wyona Holmes Jaffe.

-Jennie Lee Hawkins Holmes

(Author's note: Jennie Lee died on my birthday, January 27, 1978, at the age of 87, one year after I began to tell her story.)

Table of Contents

Chapter 1: Jennie the Child............... 11
Chapter 2: Jennie the Woman........... 29
Chapter 3: Jennie the Wife............... 33
Chapter 4: Jennie the Mother
  -on the ranch...................... 39
Chapter 5: Jennie the Mother
  - in the city......................... 49
Chapter 6: Jennie the Mother
  -the empty nest................... 63
Chapter 7: Jennie the grandmother.. 75
Appendix.. 93
Bibliography...................................... 122
Index.. 124
About the author............................. 136

The pioneers of these early days in the Verde Valley found the soil rich and loamy and they were soon growing crops of corn, barley, wheat, and vegetables and putting in fruit orchards. The river, at that time, was shallow with many stagnant pools breeding mosquitoes. Malaria was prevalent among the settlers until later years when the floods cleared the channel and the water flowed freely. Irrigation systems were formed from the Verde River, Oak Creek, Clear Creek, and Beaver Creek so that the valley had plenty of water for farming.

CHAPTER 1

Jennie the Child

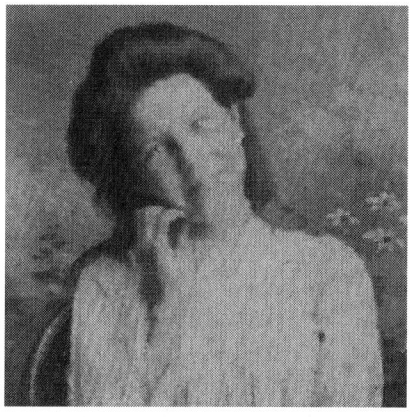

In April 1875, my grandparents, William Henry and Harriet Hawkins, joined a wagon train in Missouri with the intention of going to the gold fields of California. They were accompanied by many other families, including the James Bristows, the Burfords, the Dickinsons, the Letts, the Davidsons, the Hutchinsons, the Tom Smiths, the James Humans, and the Pleasant Bristows.[1] When the wagon train reached the Verde Valley of Arizona Territory, the settlers, seeing the rich soil and the trees growing lush and green at the edge of the Verde River, decided to go no further.

Grandpa and Grandma Hawkins homesteaded on the property that is now Dead Horse Ranch State Park in Cottonwood, which is near Tuzigoot National Monument. When they started homesteading, Tuzigoot Indian ruin was just a rocky hill located on the edge of their property. William Henry Hawkins, Sr. took an active part in the community. In October 1876, he was on the election board of the Upper Verde Valley with J. O. Bristow and Francis Wingfield.

[1.] Recorded in <u>Pioneer Stories of Arizona's Verde Valley</u>, P. 194; also in <u>Those Early Days</u>, P. 178

Exhibit at Dead Horse Ranch State Park. This is where the elder Hawkins family settled in 1875.

By the time the Hawkins' settled in the valley, most of the Apache Indians, who had surrendered in April 1873, had been taken to San Carlos Indian Reservation. However, there were still a few around that would come to the ranches for food. The settlers were afraid of the Indians, as they were never sure if they were friendly or hostile.

The settlement of Camp Verde was well established by 1880. Fort Verde, which was built to protect the settlers in 1871-1873, was abandoned by the soldiers in 1891. It is now the site of the Fort Verde Historical Museum in Camp Verde.

At the time the elder Hawkins family came to the Verde Valley, the territorial capital was located at Tucson. The following excerpt from the Weekly Arizona Miner *from Prescott dated January 22, 1875 gives some indication of how the people in Prescott were feeling about the territorial capital issue. Prescott did get the honor of having the capital in 1877; then two years later it was moved to Phoenix.*

Weekly Arizona Miner (Prescott)
January 22, 1875
Capital Removal

"The telegraph tells us that the good people of Phoenix are greatly exercised over the Capital removal question. They think their town is entitled to be the future Capital of Arizona, by right divine, water right or some other right. The people of Tucson are not a whit behind in their capital aspirations. They have it now and mean to keep it.

Prescott people have hopes that the capital will come back here, to its old location, and we hope it will, as, in our poor judgment, Prescott is the proper place for the capital. It is the largest American town in the Territory and, of course, the healthiest. Then, we consider it to be the heart of the best mining, grazing and timber sections of the Territory, so, we say to the Legislature, give us back the capital and so aid us to raise Arizona to the position that belongs to her among other great geographical divisions of the Republic. Prescott people would feel duly grateful for the passage of a bill giving them the Capital, and would, thereby, be nerved to nobler deeds than any of those for which they are already famous.

As the pioneer town of Northern Arizona, Prescott has well and nobly done her duty in upholding the banner of civilization against barbarous foes, and conquering from their grasp the fairest, richest and best portion of the Territory. We, therefore, ask Legislators to think of Prescott and her claims when voting upon the questions." **Source: Capitol Archives**

When my grandfather died in 1883 (according to an article in the Jerome Reporter, August 1, 1901, he died by drinking poison by mistake), it was up to the remaining men in the family to help their mother with the ranching.[2] At that time, there were only

---

[2.] See Appendix #3 for complete newspaper article from Verde Independent March 13th, 2013.

four brothers left alive. Because my Uncle Lee was occupied with his dental practice in Jerome, he couldn't help with the ranch; therefore, this task was left to his brothers Tom, Emery and William, my father. When my grandmother died in 1895, the ranch was divided among my father, Tom and Emery.[3]

The other sons in the family met with early deaths, as was common in those hard pioneer days. John was killed when he was thrown from a horse at age 18 in 1876.[4] Erastus died suddenly in 1880 from some unknown cause. James was shot and killed in the line of duty as a peace officer in Jerome in 1891. He was killed by a man by the name of Tom Gallagher, who was tried and convicted and sent to prison. He was pardoned and died in Tucson a short time later.[5]

My Uncle Tom's life was cut short by a tragic accident in July 1901. He and Ed Walker were returning from locating mining claims in the Cherry Creek area when they came to Mockingbird Creek, which was running full from a recent rain. Ed persuaded Tom not to cross the horse and buggy through the current, so Tom unhitched the horse and tried to cross the stream on horseback. The horse slipped and fell on Tom and he was drowned. Uncle Tom was to have been married to Rhoda Marr of Aultman on the following August 10. He had been building a house for her and had almost finished it when he died. (See Appendix # 5 for newspaper article from <u>Jerome Reporter</u>, August 1, 1901.)

[3.] See Appendix #4 for land transactions by Hawkins family and description of land that the ranch was located on.
[4.] John Hawkins was the first person to be buried in the Cottonwood Cemetery according to <u>Pioneer Stories of Arizona's Verde Valley</u>, p. 143, and also <u>Those Early Days</u>, p. 146. I located several of the Hawkins family graves, but did not find John's.
[5.] The shooting of James Hawkins was also reported by the <u>Arizona Weekly Miner</u> from Prescott on Jan 14, 1891 p, 3 column 3 and again April 22, 1891, p 2 column 4. Source: Jerome Historical Society.

One of the settlers that came to the Verde Valley in the same wagon train with the Hawkins family in 1875 told of some of the hardships they endured in the crossing from Missouri. Mrs. Charles Dickinson, who was 12 years old at the time of the journey, wrote:

"One night in Kansas there came up an awful storm. The cattle broke away from the guards and got in a grain field and destroyed lots of grain. The men had to pay $40 damage.

We got word that Indians were killing all travelers, so that night they corralled all wagons in a circle but the Indians did not molest us. Sometimes it would be a long time the women could not do any washing on account of not being able to find a place where there was plenty of feed and water for our stock. We also learned to wear our clothes un-ironed.

For meat we had buffalo meat and buffalo calf meat to eat.

My father (P. W. Burford) drove our milk cows with their calves. The calves got all the milk in the daytime but at night we tied them up so we always got all the morning milk. My mother strained the milk in a big churn that was kept in front of the wagon and the motion of the wagon churned the milk and we had butter all the time..."

From: <u>Pioneer Stories of Arizona's Verde Valley</u>, p. 22.

The following story about the Hawkins boys (Jennie's uncles) is an excerpt from <u>Pioneer Stories of Arizona's Verde Valley</u>, as told by W. A. Jordan who came to the Verde Valley in 1880:

"...*The Indians broke camp next morning and started on down the valley. Just at a turn in the road where there was a clump of sycamore and alder trees, they met Tom Hawkins, then a half-grown kid, riding the Hawkins' race horse, Charlie, and carrying a basket of eggs to market at the mining camp (later named Jerome). Tom was scared stiff at the blood-smeared leader and after they had passed him with a few friendly 'How's' he set down the basket of eggs and going back over the Peck's Lake trail, he put old Charlie to his best speed, and going two miles to the Indians' one, he got home and told his brother, Emery, that there was a band of warriors coming before an Indian was in sight. Emery grabbed a gun and threw it across the front fence all ready to shoot on sight, but the Indian was more alert than he and again waved his paper, shouting as before, 'Don't shoot, don't shoot.'*

...The settlers were in no danger from this friendly band of hunters, but they were so wrought up over the stories of massacres and murders that the Indians themselves were in the greatest danger." **Source: *Pioneer Stories of Arizona's Verde Valley*, *p.109*.**

My Uncle Emery was a real cowboy, and he stayed in the valley and continued ranching until his health failed. He was a big, strong man, but after he was kicked in the back by a horse, his health went steadily downhill. He died when he was only 36 years old.

Uncle Lee had a flourishing dental practice in the booming mining town of Jerome. He started practicing his dentistry there at the age of 21. Some say that his first patients were horses. Although he was often chided for his lack of formal schooling in dentistry, he did eventually go to dental school and took a post-graduate course in Chicago. For about seven years he traveled around the Arizona Territory practicing his trade, but he eventually went back to Jerome.

Dr. Lee Hawkins pioneer dentist of Jerome (Photo courtesy of Jerome Historical Society).

It was there that he met and married Ethyl Carrier, the daughter of Dr. Myron Carrier, Jerome's first doctor. They were married in 1890 and had one son, Myron, who was known to be spoiled and rowdy. One of Myron's favorite tricks was to throw rocks down on the mules that were pulling the ore wagons up the steep grades of Jerome's streets. I suppose he thought it would be great fun to see the mules bolt and fall over the side of the mountain taking them or wagons and drivers with them! He died at age 21 in an accident in Hawaii.[6] Despite his son's actions, Dr. Hawkins was very well thought of and was elected president of the Arizona Dental Society in 1915.

In 1903 Lee and a man named Walter Miller brought the first automobile to the Verde Valley. It was a Franklin, and the townspeople were sure that the new-fangled contraption would never negotiate the steep grades of Jerome. Lee and Walter soon proved them wrong as the car did very well in getting around

---

[6.] According to Agnes Ramsey, her great uncle Lee Hawkins told her personally that Myron was killed while racing a motorcycle in Hawaii.

William Henry Hawkins Jr. on an outing with brother Lee and Lee's wife, Ethyl (Photo taken by Lee Hawkins courtesy of Mabel Holmes Stierwalt).

town, and soon other people began to buy automobiles, too.

Lee was apparently interested in many things. He was well known as a photographer, and he had charge of the weather bureau in Jerome for some years. This curiosity of his led him into experimenting with his dental practice. He developed a technique for filling a cavity by driving in a cactus thorn after killing the nerve in the tooth. I'm not sure how effective his method was, but you have to admit, it was different! Sometimes he would use asphalt to fill large cavities. He also invented a machine to cast inlays, but for some reason, it didn't work. He died in January 1932 and was, at that time, the longest practicing dentist in Northern Arizona. (See Appendix 9 for biographical sketch of Lee Hawkins).[7]

Although some of my father's brothers did well, none of his sisters fared too well, as they all died at a young age. Bell L. (born 1875) and Dollie (1878) both died sometime before 1895.

[7.] Many of the facts about Dr. Lee Hawkins were taken from <u>They Came to Jerome</u> by Herbert V. Young. and are used with his permission. Two pictures of Dr. Hawkins were published in <u>Those Early Days</u> p. 142, 143. One shows Dr. Hawkins with a motorcycle and one with the first automobile in Verde Valley

Records do not indicate just exactly when or why. Sarah (Mrs. James Alderson) was burned to death in 1879 at the age of 25. Louisa (Mrs. James Van Deren) died with fever in 1888 at the age of 23. Lura Belle (Mrs. Dennis Hickey) died in childbirth in 1888 at the age of 25.[8]

My parents, William Henry, Jr. and Alice Smith Hawkins, settled in the Verde Valley in 1878. Like my grandfather, my father originally intended to try his hand at working in the gold mines in California, but instead he stayed in the valley to help his parents on their ranch. I don't know why he gave up his dream of making his fortune in the gold mines, but I suppose it was because his parents had such a big ranch and needed his help.

After several years of living on his parents' ranch, my father

Photo of the old swinging bridge by the TAPCO Power plant. William and Alice's ranch was on the far side of the river just to the right of the bridge. Neither the bridge or the power plant were there when the Hawkins family lived there. According to an article in the Cottonwood Independent this bridge was torn down in February 1981. See Appendix #13 for details.

moved the family to a place of their own north of Peck's Lake on the Verde River. My parents had four children at the time they moved to their own ranch—Hattie (who was born in Illinois), Ella, Pendleton, and Virginia. The rest of us, Verde (nicknamed Verd), Mary Alice, myself, Alvin, and Bill were born later while they lived on their own ranch.[9] Another brother, Albert, was

---

[8.] See Appendix #3 -<u>Verde Independent,</u> March 10th, 2013.

born in September 1888 but lived only seven hours. At the time I was born, there was terrible flooding on the Salt and Verde Rivers in the Arizona Territory. The river near our house was a raging torrent during the time my mother was giving birth to me, and the family had to evacuate to higher ground.

Excerpt from Jennie's personal journal
November 21, 1929
"We left Prescott about 9 o'clock this a.m. We got up at 7:30, went out and had breakfast at the Palace Café again. We went to Jerome, got there at 10:30. We went up to Uncle Lee's office but he wasn't home so we didn't get to see him. We went on down to Clarkdale and across the Verde River to Tampico (TAPCO power plant) to our old home place. The old rock house was still standing. No one there but an old hen standing in the door. We came back to Clarkdale and on down to Cottonwood. Stopped and got a drink. Got over to Mayer at 2 o'clock and had dinner. The Cherry Creek road didn't seem so bad this time. Made good time. After we got over it on this side, there was an old man and his granddaughter had run off the road and couldn't get back on. So we backed up to them and pulled them back on the road. They are the only ones we met on the Cherry Road. I drove from Antelope Hill to within 4 miles of Lateral 16. Then Robert took the wheel..."

During our early childhood, my brothers and sisters and I had many happy days in spite of the harshness of our environment. We enjoyed going to Grandma Hawkins' ranch, where we played under the huge cottonwood trees along the river bank. We splashed in

Jennie and brother, Verd at the Old homestead on the Verde River

[9.] Mable Holmes Stierwalt reported that Alice returned to Springfield, Missouri to be with her mother for the birth of Ella, Pendleton, Virginia and Verde. According to the Hawkins genealogy sheet, Hattie and Verde were the only ones born in Missouri.

the water, dug in the sand, chased frogs and snakes and picked wildflowers.

Military occupation of the Verde Valley began in 1865 at the request of settlers who had established farms near the Verde River-West Clear Creek junction five miles south of present Camp Verde. There they built a crude dam and diverted water to irrigate crops, which promised to bring high prices at supply-short Prescott, then Arizona's territorial capital, and its hungry mining camps in the nearby hills.

This could have been Jennie's bedroom at Fort Verde. Photo taken at Fort Verde State Park.

The influx of Anglo and Mexican miners into the area severely disrupted the hunting and gathering economy of the Tonto Apache and Yavapai Indians.

When Indians raided Verde Valley fields for corn, settlers called on the Army for protection. The late 1860s and early 1870s saw major conflicts.

The first military post (1865) overlooked the farms at West Clear Creek. The next post, Camp Lincoln, was located one mile north of the present site and was used from 1866 to 1871. The present post was built during 1871-73. It contained more than 20 buildings arranged around a parade ground. Like other posts of the period, it never had a wall around it and was never attacked. It served as a staging base for military operations in the surrounding countryside.

During much of its life, two companies of cavalry and two of infantry were stationed at Camp Lincoln. The infantry built a wagon road west to Fort Whipple near Prescott and east to Fort Apache. Later called the Crook Trail after General George Crook, it speeded troops and supplies along the Mogollon Rim. Between 1873 and 1875, nearly 1500 Indians from various bands were placed on an 800-square-mile reserve whose headquarters were near the present town of Cottonwood. The Indians built an irrigation ditch and had 56 acres under cultivation in 1874. However, the entire population was moved to the San Carlos Reservation near Globe. The 10-day trek, which began in the cold late February of 1875, resulted in death for some of the Indians from exposure, insufficient food, and a factional fight. Some of the people returned to the Verde Valley after 1900, although the former reservation had been opened to miners and settlers in 1877.

After 1875, the Army's main concern was to keep Indians on the San Carlos and Fort Apache reservations. Indian scouts, led by Al Sieber, hunted down the renegades. An uprising in 1882 led to the last major battle with Apaches in Arizona. The insurgents were tracked to a canyon 35 miles east of Fort Verde. The ensuing Big Dry Wash fight resulted in the death or return to reservations of all renegades involved.

Camp Verde had been renamed Fort Verde in 1879 to signify permanence. Ironically, with the cessation of raids in 1882, the post became less important, and it was abandoned in 1891 to the Department of the Interior, which sold it at public auction in 1899. **(Used by permission of the Fort Verde State Historical Park.)**

We also liked to play on the rocky hill near Grandma's ranch, little realizing that this particular hill would one day be excavated to reveal Tuzigoot Indian ruin. Many times we found pieces of Indian pottery, and one of my brothers once found a pot intact with human hair inside.

Tuzigoot (Apache for "Crooked Water") is the remnant of a Sinaguan village built between 1125 and 1400 AD. It crowns the summit of a long ridge that rises 120 feet above the Verde Valley. The original pueblo was two stories high in places and had 77 ground-floor rooms. There were few exterior doors; entry was by way of ladders through openings in the roofs. The village began as a small

Tuzigoot as it looked when Jennie and her brothers and sisters played on it. It was excavated in 1933-34 by the University of Arizona. Photo courtesy of National Park Service at Tuzigoot National Monument.

cluster of rooms that were inhabited by about 50 persons for a hundred years. In the 1200s the population doubled again as refugee farmers, fleeing drought in outlying areas, settled here. **(Used with permission from National Park Service.)**

Tuzigoot as it looks today.

(Jennie left no specific remembrances of her school days in the Verde Valley, but following are some stories from people that could possibly have been classmates. In any event, these schools were, no doubt, very similar to the one Jennie attended.)

Don Willard told this story about early Verde Valley schools in Those Early Days, *p. 202: "...After we moved to Camp Verde, I went to the old two-room school house. Later I attended the one-room school at Cottonwood with all eight grades, one teacher and an average of 16 or 18 pupils. Boys were required to carry wood for the big stove and bring drinking water from the well on a nearby farm. This was kept on a shelf in an open bucket with one dipper hanging beside for all to use. In those days, we walked to school and carried our lunch in a pail, which was sometimes an emptied tobacco tin. Strange as it may seem, we had teachers who were able to get across to those who were willing to learn, not only covering the subjects in our text books, but I believe also many of the lessons of life. As I look back I am glad we did not realize we were underprivileged..."*

Clara Purtyman, an early pioneer of the Oak Creek area, tells this story in <u>Those Early Days</u>, p. 72: "Before we had a school in Oak Creek Canyon, we had to move to Red Rock to go to school. I went to the first school ever held there in 1891. I was five years old and Miss Minnie Maxwell was the first teacher there and also my first teacher. It did not make any difference about my age because I was needed to make up the attendance so they could have a school. This school was a little cabin on the Henry Schuerman place. The teacher used to make me a bed on a bench and I would take a little nap in the afternoon because it was too far for me to walk home by myself. We always had to take our lunch. We studied arithmetic, reading, language, spelling, geography, and copybooks. They were books in which you wrote underneath the words in the book. This is how we were taught writing. Sometimes when the snow was deep, Dad made overshoes for us by wrapping gunnysacks around our shoes. Our feet sure kept warm in those homemade overshoes..."
(Used by permission of Sedona Westerners from their book, <u>Those Early Days.</u>)

My brothers and sisters and I attended school in a one-room schoolhouse with a teacher whose salary was paid for by all the parents of the students.[10]

When I was about seven years old, my mother, who had never been very strong, got sick enough that she couldn't continue doing the hard work on the ranch. My father sold the ranch and we moved into the old barracks at the "Post" (the settlers name for Fort Verde) so Mother could be near a doctor. However, we only stayed there three months. Uncle Emery had bought a ranch at Clear Creek near Fort Verde and asked my father to run it for him. We moved to the ranch and lived there about a year before Mother's health got worse again.

My father took her to Flagstaff where the Arizona State Hospital was then located. As I look back on the kind of life

---

[10.] This was probably the Middle Verde School, but there is no concrete data to back this up.

my mother had, I don't wonder that her mind gave way along with her physical health. She endured a covered wagon journey across the country, floods, Indian scares, the constant fear of death or injury to her children, hard physical labor on the ranch, and many hardships that we will never know about.

When it was determined that there was no help for my mother in Flagstaff, Papa took her to a new hospital in Phoenix. (This was the present-day Arizona State Hospital.) My mother was only there a short time before she died on July 18, 1900. I never saw her again after Papa took her to Flagstaff. I was only nine years old at the time Mother died, and I was a very sad little girl for a while.

After Mother died, Papa moved us to Phoenix to live with my married sister, Hattie, near Five Points (the intersection of 7th Avenue, Grand Avenue, and Van Buren). My brothers Bill and Alvin, my sister Mary Alice and I attended Five Points School near the canal, which was called the "town ditch" in those days.[11] We had many good times swimming in the old "town ditch."

My fourth grade teacher at Five Points School was a sister to the first grade teacher I had in the Verde Valley. Reverend R. A. Windes was my Sunday school teacher. He was the minister of the Baptist Church in the Verde Valley and also taught at our school there. Reverend Windes baptized my mother in the Verde River some years before she died.

William Henry Hawkins Jr. 1903

[11.] In November 1903 Mary Alice married Edd McAnally when she was only 14 years old.

(Emery and Thomas Hawkins sold Reverend Windes 80 acres of land in April 1896).[12]

> *A year before William and Harriet Hawkins came to Arizona (1874) the population of the Territory of Arizona was about 11,000. When Jennie moved to Phoenix in 1900, the population of Phoenix was 5,544.* **(Source: <u>Arizona, Its People and Resources,</u> p. 21)**

In the winter of 1902, Bill, Alvin and I came down with the measles. Hattie had to leave us alone, as she had to go to work at the Phoenix Laundry. Dr. Bell, who was a well-known doctor in Phoenix, came to the house every day to check on us. One day when he was there, I complained of being hungry, so he warmed up a can of pork and beans and fed us. He also warmed up the coffee that Hattie made that morning and gave each of us a cup of it. Dr. Bell's kindness left an impression that stayed with me for the rest of my life.

> *The settling of Phoenix in the Salt River Valley was wholly dependent on the available water supply, which was left, at first, to the whims of nature. The farmers soon realized that in order to have dependable water they needed to control the water supply; therefore, they began to establish irrigation systems.*
> *1867—First canal company*
> *1880—Nine additional canals*
> *1897-99—Drought years*
> *1900—Flash flood that washed out all diversion dams on the Salt and Verde Rivers*
> *1902—First Reclamation Act passed*
> *1905—Roosevelt Dam started*
> *1912—Roosevelt Dam completed*
> **(Source: <u>Arizona – Its People and Resources</u>, p. 121**

---

[12] See Appendix #4, Land Transactions.

*National Bank of Arizona Building, Phoenix.
(From 1916 Post Card.)*

Not long after coming to Phoenix, Papa opened a restaurant at 5th Avenue and Washington. (This was directly across the street from where my son Bob eventually had his electrical contracting business, DeBerge and Holmes Electric. He began working for DeBerge Electric in 1941 and bought into the business in 1946.) Papa couldn't make a go of the restaurant, so he got a job delivering the mail from Phoenix to Arlington, about 50 miles west of Phoenix. His "mail truck" was a horse-drawn wagon. Sometimes I would go with my father on his route and can particularly remember the times when the Agua Fria River was flooded. Papa urged the horse to run all the way across so as not to get caught in the quicksand. It was scary to feel the rushing water all around the wagon, and I was always glad when we got to the other side without being washed downstream or getting stuck in the sand.

We stopped at the Cold Water store owned by Bill Moore, picked up the mail, and went on to Arlington, where Papa lived between trips to Phoenix. I stayed with the Wetzler family because my father lived in a tent and didn't have room for me. My brothers were still staying with Hattie in Phoenix.

The mail wagon that William drove between Arlington and Phoenix for 4 years. William is standing on the porch in the photo. (Photo courtesy of William Henry Holmes).

Will Wetzler operated the store and post office at Arlington. I eventually went to live with the Wetzlers instead of going back and forth to Phoenix.

When Papa made the return trip to Phoenix, he stopped at some of the farmers' places and picked up cream and milk to take to the Maricopa Creamery in Tempe. (It was located southeast of the Hayden Mill on the south bank of the Salt River on old 8th Street, between Rural and McClintock. The building still exists.) He dropped me off at Five Points while he continued the round trip between Tempe and Arlington. He worked this route for four years.

My early years of hard work on the ranch, the loss of my mother, and the responsibility of taking care of my brothers was inevitably preparing me for the next phase of my life, that of becoming a woman.

CHAPTER 2

Jennie the Woman

As I was entering my teen years, circumstances in my family brought about a number of changes in my life. My sister Ella had married Hugh Brewer, a butcher from Jerome, in July 1895, and they moved to Colorado four years later. In 1903, at the age of 24, she died giving birth to her third child. Later, Hugh brought their two small children, Walter and Blanche, to Hattie to take care of. Since Hattie obviously had more responsibility than she could handle at this time, Papa moved Bill, Alvin, and me to a house in Buckeye. He was now working there in Riley Johnson's store. I was just 13 years old, but my father must have thought I was old enough to take care of him and my two brothers.

Jennie about 1910 (Photo courtesy of Mary Holmes Olvey).

I really thought I was grown up keeping house for my father and brothers. I cooked on an old wood stove and did the laundry on a washboard just like all the other women. Like most young girls, I occasionally longed to have some fun, so one day when my brother Verd came to visit from Cottonwood, we decided to

The Main Street of Buckeye 1908. (Photo courtesy of William Holmes.)

go on a picnic with some friends, Rube Woods and his sister. We hitched up the horse and buggy and went to the Haynes Mine, an old gold mine north of Buckeye. After we had eaten our picnic lunch, Verd and Rube climbed down in the mine shaft, which looked to be about 150 feet deep. Verd warned us girls not to follow them, but we did anyway.

At the bottom of the ladder was a dark tunnel. We began to explore the tunnel, but I got scared and started back up the ladder. When I was about half way up, something hit me hard on the shoulder. I almost fell off the ladder! Verd and Rube heard me cry out and thought I was falling down the shaft. They held their arms out to catch me, but it was my little brother Bill they caught, not me. I didn't know it was Bill until I got to the top and some other friends that were there told me it was Bill who fell. We were sure he had been killed by the fall! We sent down the bucket that the miners used to bring ore out of the mine, and we brought the unconscious Bill out of the shaft in it. In the meantime, someone went ten miles into town to get Dr. Thayer, and he arrived a short time later. He determined that Bill had broken both his right arm and leg in two places. I helped the doctor set the broken bones and also helped him sew up a bad cut on Bill's face.

The doctor sent Bill home with Verd and me, and I took care of him till he got well. He was unconscious for two weeks, and I had to feed him with a spoon all that time. Dr. Thayer said I was a pretty good nurse even if I was only 14 years old. Bill fell down the mine on February 18, and it was May before he was completely well again.

One day, while Bill's leg was still in a cast, he decided he wanted to go visit a friend. I tried to tell him he wasn't able to go anywhere, but he insisted on going anyway. Bill propped his leg up in his wagon and pushed with the other one. He managed to get there and back with no problem. I was really worried and was very much relieved when he came back to the house.

About a year after Bill's accident, tragedy struck again! In June 1906, while I was across the street visiting neighbors, our house caught on fire. The neighbor shouted, "Jennie, your house is on fire!" I ran to the door just in time to see the house burn to the ground. We lost everything we owned! Papa built a little one-room house for us, but I only stayed there for several months before going to stay with sister Mary in Phoenix.

The events leading up to this point in my life were to directly affect my future. Not having a home to call my own and living with other people naturally resulted in a longing for a home of my own. Therefore, when a young man came into my life, I was more than ready to begin looking forward to my role as "Jennie the wife."

Buckeye Hotel 1908. (Photo courtesy of William Holmes.)

Robert and Jennie's wedding picture.
November 18, 1906
(Photo courtesy of Mabel Holmes Stierwalt).

CHAPTER 3

Jennie the Wife

Just before going to Phoenix, I had met a young man by the name of John Robert Holmes (known to everyone as Robert). We met at one of the community dances where Robert played the violin. It was love at first sight for both of us—I was 15 and Robert was 25 years old. We got to know each other better through the Wetzler Family. Ada Wetzler, who was Robert's sister, was sister-in-law to Will Wetzler, the family I had stayed with when my father was driving the mail route between Phoenix and Arlington.

After I moved to Phoenix to live with my sister Mary, Robert came to visit and asked me to marry him. I was only too glad to accept his proposal, as I really felt we were meant for each other. We were married that fall on November 18, 1906. I became a mother the day of my marriage,

Invitation to one of the community dances. Courtesy of William Holmes.

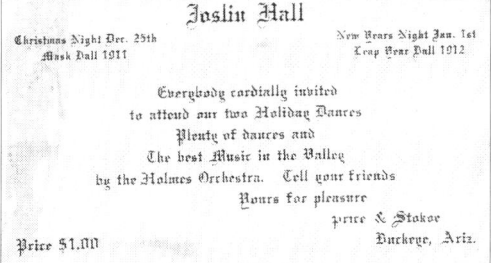

Robert and his violin. (Photo courtesy of Mary Holmes Olvey).

as Robert had a five-year-old daughter, Myrtle Edna, from a previous marriage. His first wife, Alice Henry Holmes, had died several months before we were married.

<u>Excerpt from Jennie's personal journal</u>
November 18, 1937 (Written on Robert and Jennie's 31st Wedding Anniversary)

"Thirty-one years of perfect bliss. That is more than most married people can say. It has been different today than it was 31 years ago today. In 1906 it was stormy on November 18th, the day we were married at sister Mary's house down on Buckeye Road and 9th Avenue. We drove to Robert's father's home 18 miles west of St. Johns where we stayed that night (Saturday). On Sunday we drove to Arlington where we lived one year, farming, then moved back to the old ranch. There we lived till 1923. We have been here in Phoenix 14 years. Our kiddies are all married but Bill. He will be 16 years old next month. We have four grandchildren, three girls, one boy. We are happy today and healthy. Mabel, Roy, and kiddies (Madeline and Mary Belle), Vi, Wyona, Billie, Robert and I enjoyed supper together tonight. Sister (daughter Mary) and Chuck are in Panama; Pinkie, Merle and Jimmie are in Los Angeles; Bob is working at the Bartlett Dam. Robert took the kiddies home. It is a beautiful moonlight night and warm. Billie is busy studying. I have a backache today. Hope to live another 31 years."

John Robert Holmes 16 years old. (Photo courtesy of Mabel Holmes Stierwalt).

I was very proud of my new husband. He was born in England and was an honest, hard-working man. He had a deep appreciation of the freedoms and opportunities offered in America because of the

Robert's parents, Mary and James Holmes. Taken about 1880 in England. (Photo courtesy of William Holmes)

hardships he and his family had endured in England. Robert attended a school in Dalton-in-Furness, England, run by the Church of England. The schools operated by the church were considered the private schools—the others were the "public" schools. Each year, the students were given a test and the one scoring the highest was given a scholarship to one of the "Public Schools of Higher Learning." In 1895, the year Robert was 14 years old, he and two of his classmates tied as the highest-scoring students in their school. One of the students immigrated to Australia, Robert immigrated to America, and the other one stayed to take advantage of the scholarship and eventually became a member of the House of Commons.

Robert's father, James, was an iron miner and he left England to escape the oppression by the mine owners. He also had developed miners' consumption or asthma and was advised to go to a dry climate for his health. He and Robert's oldest sister came to the United States first, and then Robert and his mother and two sisters followed later in 1895. They came by steerage, the lowest accommodation for passengers on a ship. The women were housed on one side of the ship and the men on the other. Robert, being the only male in the family, and being 14 years old, was faced with the prospect of going into the men's section alone. He refused to go until his mother bought him a pack of cigarettes and said, "Now, you are a man!" When they arrived at the port of entry at Ellis Island, Robert had an eye infection, and the whole family was kept in quarantine until the infection cleared up. When they were allowed to leave, the family traveled across the country by train to Phoenix. From there they went by horse-drawn wagon to the ranch near Buckeye that Robert's father was homesteading.

Mabel Holmes Stierwalt remembers her grandfather James talking about the way it was in England—the miners had to tip their hats to the "lords" or whatever the owners of the mines were called. One day, when they were driving down the road near their ranch in their horse-drawn wagon, she noticed that each person they passed tipped his hat and that her grandfather returned the gesture. "I thought you said you didn't tip your hat to any man," said Mabel. "Yes," said Grandfather, "but here everyone does it because they want to, not because they have to."

Robert's mother, Mary, Sisters, Sarah, Agnes and Ada. Robert is on far right. Taken about 1885 in England. (Photo courtesy of William Holmes.)

The following is an excerpt from a news story written by Jay Brashear, <u>Phoenix Gazette</u> staff writer, in 1952. It was a story about I. H. Parkman, who was instrumental in establishing Buckeye's historical museum. He came to Buckeye the same year Robert and his mother and sisters did, so he must have seen the very same sights and had the same feelings that 14-year-old Robert must have had when he saw Buckeye for the first time.

"Buckeye, November 14—The year was 1895.
An apprehensive quiet had settled on the flaming Arizona territory. But it was like the stunned, smoky quiet that follows the deathly roar of a hammer-fanned six gun. The Indians were peaceful and the outlaws a little less bold. But honest men kept their Colts and Winchesters loaded and within easy reach—just in case the quiet didn't last. It was on a soft March day in 1895 that I. H. Parkman, then a bright-eyed lad of 15, rode into Buckeye on an open wagon after an overnight journey from Phoenix, some 30 miles to the east. As the wagon bounced over the bumpy, dusty road, the boy got his first look at Buckeye—a general store and post office combined, a saloon, and two dwelling houses..."

Robert and I spent the first year of our marriage on a rented ranch near Arlington. It was not easy to make a living on a ranch in those days, and we soon moved to the homestead with Robert's parents, James and Mary Holmes. When we had been there about six months, his mother was found to have cancer of the liver and had to have an operation. She died three weeks after the operation on August 19, 1907. Robert's father became more ill after her death, and I took care of him while Robert found odd jobs to make a living. At times, the only cash coming in was the money he received for playing the violin at the community dances twice a month. After Robert's mother died, his father gave him 80 acres of the homestead, and he built a house for us there. At this time, Robert was working his 80 acres and his father's ranch at the same time. When his father could no longer stay alone, we moved him to a small house near us on our ranch, which meant that I now had the full responsibility for caring for my ailing father-in-law.

The old homestead – 1919. Robert and Bobbie are sitting on the plow on the right. The homestead was located near the confluence of the Salt and Gila Rivers, 12 miles west of St. Johns Indian Mission. The Salt and Gila Rivers come together at about the first meridian (115th Avenue). The homestead was on the Gila River and the brush dams were on the Salt River. The family sometimes referred to the homestead as being at St. Johns and sometimes Cashion.

Robert used his 80 acres to raise alfalfa and wheat—but his 80 acres didn't stay 80 acres! When the Gila River flooded, it sometimes washed away ten acres at a time! During one of these floods, a large haystack was in danger of being washed away by the river and all available hands worked hard to save it. They managed to get it moved just in time as they watched the river cut away the bank right next to it!

During these early years of our marriage, we had many difficult times. We lost, not only Robert's mother, but also my little brother Alvin who died in July of 1910. He had a sore on his nose that became infected and turned to blood poisoning. In spite of this, we looked forward to starting our own family. It didn't start out too well as we lost two little boys, George in 1907 and Henry in 1908. Our first living child was born in 1910.

CHAPTER 4

Jennie the Mother
--On the Ranch--

*Mabel, Mary, Bobbie, and Pinkie with Jennie--1917.
(Photo courtesy of Mary Holmes Olvey).*

During the first four years of my marriage, I was very busy taking care of my sick father-in-law, my step-daughter, Myrtle, and Lillian Russell, Robert's niece, who was being raised by Robert's mother. Lillian came to live with us after his mother died. It was during these first four years that I lost two baby boys, George and Henry. But I was to have joyous times, too, as I gave birth to my five living children during the next eleven years.

Myrtle, 3 years old and Lillian Russell, 8 years old. Lillian was Robert's sister, Sara's eldest daughter. (Photo courtesy of William Henry Holmes).

My oldest daughter Mabel Belle, was born on September 10, 1910. Robert and I had a disagreement about what to name her—I wanted to name her "Jennie," but Robert said he had one "Jennie" and didn't need another one! Two years later, Mary Alice (nicknamed Sis or Sister) was born on July 11, 1912—the year Arizona became a state. I guess I should have named her "State," but it wouldn't have been the kindest thing to saddle her with such a strange name! When Mrs. Davis, the midwife, was helping me deliver Mary, she held her up to give her a swat and predicted that Mary would be the "cat" of the family. I don't know exactly what she meant unless she was predicting that Mary would be the one to wander far from home. If so, the prediction came true, as Mary became a missionary and went to far-away South America.

Mary (left), cousin Verna and Mabel Right --1922. (Photo courtesy of Mary Holmes Olvey).

Our first living son, Robert Ullock (Bobbie), came along 22 months after Mary on August 13, 1914. "Ullock" was my husband's mother's maiden name. World War I started the day after Bobbie was born. James Wilson, our second son, was born three years later on June 12, 1917. He was nicknamed "Pinkie" because of his blonde hair which almost looked pink. He was born in Phoenix at the home of Mrs. Davis, the midwife who also helped me with Mabel and Mary. Our youngest, William Henry (Billie) was born on December 16, 1921. We named him after my father, which made Billie the third William Henry in three generations.

Excerpt from Jennie's personal journal   *January 6, 1937*

"Twenty four years ago today (1913) was the coldest day of the year. 24 years ago, today, Robert and I and Sister (Mary), then 6 months old, drove to Phoenix from the ranch in the buggy. We nearly froze to death going home in the afternoon. We stopped on the desert and made a fire to warm us. Poor little Sis was frozen stiff and blue. Nearly scared us to death. I had to rub her to get the life back into her..."

Bobbie, 3 years old --1917. (Photo courtesy of Mary Holmes Olvey).

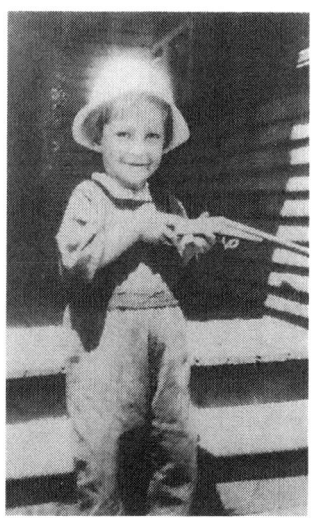

James Wilson (Pinkie) 2 years old 1919. William Henry (Billie) 2 years old 1923. (Photo courtesy of Mary Holmes Olvey).

Myrtle and Jennie about 1920. (Photo courtesy of Mary Holmes Olvey).

I have already mentioned Myrtle Edna (Bea) who was five years old when Robert and I married. She called me "Mama" right away, and she was like my own daughter. When Myrtle was 17 years old, we sent her to Tempe Normal School to study to be a teacher. While she was attending school from 1917 to 1919 she met Lawrence Conley. Myrtle showed up at our ranch one day introducing him as her new husband. Robert and I wanted her to finish school, so we weren't too happy about her marriage. But, what was done was done, so the two of them went to Liberty, Arizona, to live near Lawrence's folks. About a year later, our first grandchild, Robert Lawrence (Larry) was born.

Myrtle died tragically when she was only 21 years old—the same day our youngest, Billie, was born. She was expecting her second child and began to miscarry after going horseback riding. Robert took her to the hospital in Phoenix in critical condition on December 16. Later that day, I went into labor and sent the children to the school teacher's house to stay. I sent someone to fetch Dr. Thayer. (At that time, we lived on Meridian #1, now 115th Avenue, near the school in Cashion.) The midwife arrived to help, too. Little Pinkie thought he was going to help out by chopping some wood and a chip flew in his eye, injuring it seriously. Robert came back from the hospital after Myrtle died just in time to be there when Billie was born but had to return to Phoenix immediately with Pinkie to try to save his eye. Robert was so upset by all these things happening that he didn't want to look at the new baby for a long time (See Appendix 15).

In spite of all the grief and hurt, life must go on. Robert was soon engrossed with the enormous task of keeping the ranch going and we all settled back into our daily routine.

Wash Day on the Ranch

The night before wash day, hitch the horses to the sleigh. Fill two barrels of water from the river.
Add ashes to the water to make the water soft and let sit over night. The next morning, skim the ashes off the top. Build a fire and bring water to boiling. Put water and soap in one tub for boiling white clothes.

One tub for scrubbing and another tub for rinsing. Scrub clothes on wash board and put in boiling water. Stir with broom handle stick. Rinse. Hang on fence to dry

A big part of the struggle to make a living for the farmers and ranchers in this part of Arizona in the early 1900's was keeping the irrigation systems that originated on the Salt and Gila Rivers in working order. Shortly after coming to this valley in 1895, Robert and his father joined with the other ranchers in building brush dams on these two rivers. The dams diverted water for their farms and ranches into canals they had dug themselves. Many of these canals followed the original ones made by the Hohokam Indians. It was hard work keeping the dams and canals in working order. Every time the river flooded, it would wash away the dams, and it would take a month of cutting trees and hauling rock to rebuild them.

During the ten years after Robert's mother died, his dad had been getting worse with his lung disease. At first he stayed on his ranch, but as he needed more care, we brought him to live with us. On September 6, 1916, Grandpa started gasping for air and wanted me to carry him outside so he could breathe better. One of the children ran to get a neighbor to help me while Myrtle rode the blue mare five miles to get Robert who was working on the dam. The neighbor and I carried Grandpa outside, but then he wanted to go back inside again. He just kept gasping for air—he finally died in my arms.

Robert and Pinkie 1919. (Photo courtesy of Mary Holmes Olvey).

The year 1919 was a bad year for us. In February the whole family had the flu. Then in May, Robert and Mary both had typhoid fever. Robert was down with it four weeks and Mary, two. On June 28, we went to visit my sister Mary in Los

Angeles. We also went to visit my father, who had moved to Long Beach some time after Robert and I were married. Robert developed an infection in both legs as a result of his recent bout with typhoid fever. He had an operation on one of his legs where the doctors scraped the shin bone and inserted a piece of silver over the bone. After two months in California, we returned to Arizona, and Robert realized that he couldn't do the heavy work on the ranch so we rented it to Mr. and Mrs. Mitchell.

We moved into Grandpa Holmes' old two-room wooden shack on the ranch, where we managed to scrape by on the money from the rental and from the chickens we raised. We ate an awful lot of chicken and eggs during this hard time, and poor Mabel got so tired of eating chicken that she had an aversion to it for a long time after that. Cousin Wallace McAnally, sister Mary's son, stayed with us, and he helped out a lot by hunting rabbits, dove, and quail to put food on the table.

In 1921 Robert took a job as deputy sheriff offered to him by his sister Agnes' husband, John G. Montgomery, who was sheriff of Maricopa County at that time. Robert was in charge of guarding the bootleggers and once let two of them get away.

Bobblie and the old work mule 1919. (Photo courtesy of Mary Holmes Olvey).

About this time, we sold the ranch and rented a house near the school in the Cashion area. The school was called the St. John's School District and there was no settlement near it at the time we lived there. I was glad to be near the school, as I was anxious for my children to have a good education. They got off to a pretty good start with Mabel's first grade teacher, Mrs. Roberts, taking a special interest in her. She often took Mabel home with her because she enjoyed giving her extra tutoring. Mrs. Roberts wanted to make a teacher out of Mabel, and she succeeded, as she later taught school at Cashion for 20 years. When Mabel started to school in 1916, classes were held in the old schoolhouse, but a new one was being built nearby. At recess one day, the kids were running and playing at the site of the new schoolhouse. Mabel started walking on the beams where the new floor was being laid, and she slipped and fell across one of the beams. When the teacher brought her home, you couldn't tell it was Mabel because her face was so swollen and black and blue. Like to scared me to death! Bobbie and Pinkie also had Mrs. Roberts to get them started in school. It wasn't long before she had Pinkie doing third grade work while he was still in the first grade.

Mary and Mabel studying 1918. (Photo courtesy of Mary Holmes Olvey.)

<u>Excerpt from Jennie's personal journal</u>
January 9, 1929
"I was out in the back yard watering the trees when I looked up and saw a one-year-old baby walking down the railroad track. I heard a train coming so I ran and grabbed the baby. I asked it where its mama was and all it could say was, "Mama." I looked around wondering what to do with this lost child. I then saw a young woman running down the track toward me. Of course, it was the baby's mother very much relieved to see her child in my arms. She said she had gone to the store and the baby had followed her."

*Bobbie and Pinkie 1918.
(Photo courtesy of Mary Holmes Olvey).*

I was also determined that my children would have the opportunity to take music lessons. When Mary started school, she and Mabel both took piano lessons from a teacher in Cashion. They practiced on a piano belonging to a couple of widow ladies who built a home on the hill across the river. They had brought a concert piano with them from Denver, and eventually they gave it to Mabel and Mary. Our house was small, but we were proud to have this piano in our crowded front room. One of the proudest days of our lives was when our two little girls played the piano in a school exercise when they were about eight and six years old. We thought they were just about the smartest kids around! We took the piano with us when we moved to Phoenix. Mary then took violin lessons, and she and Mabel played duets.

After Robert's operation on his leg, he knew he would never be able to get back into ranching again, so we moved to Phoenix in March of 1923. This move brought about a great number of changes in our lives.

Robert and Jennie with their 1917 Ford. Notation from Jennie's notebook of family records: " Robert bought a Ford car in February 1918 for $423. It burned up in May 1918 and he bought another one and it cost $600."
(Photo courtesy of Mary Holmes Olvey).

<u>Excerpt from Jennie's personal journal</u>
January 5, 1929

"I did a big washing with Bobbie's help—took me till 1:00 to finish. The girls had gone to Buckeye with Edna (Wetzler) that morning and got home about 4:30. They helped get supper then we went to town to take the boys to play basketball at the YMCA. The new Orpheum Theater opened tonight where Phoenix's first talking movies were shown. There were five big spotlights on it and it was beautiful. It was so cold walking on the streets. We saw a blind man with a wife and two little girls. He was playing a harp and his wife was holding a hat out for money. I felt so sorry for them. I bought some popcorn for Billie. I tried to find a teakettle to buy but couldn't find one."

CHAPTER 5

Jennie the Mother
--in the City--

Robert and Jennie and four of their five children: Billie, Pinkie, Bobbie and Mabel. Mary and her husband, Chuck had gone to Venezuela, South America to be missionaries in 1937.
(Photo courtesy of Violet Hopkins Holmes.)

After we moved to Phoenix at 1746 W. Buchanan Street, we missed the freedom of the wide open spaces on the ranch, but there was no doubt that life was a lot easier in the city. We quickly settled into a comfortable routine of daily chores and responsibilities, but we also had time to visit with family and friends. In fact, there was hardly a day that went by that we didn't have visitors of some kind. [13.]

In 1923 in Phoenix:
---It took first class mail three days to go from New York to Phoenix.
---It took 14 hours to go by auto from San Diego to Phoenix.
---Phoenix Union High School had 1,827 students.
---Phoenix had 17 elementary schools.
Source: ***Arizona and Its People and Resources, p. 21***

The house on west Buchanan Street.
(Photo courtesy William Henry Holmes).

Our red brick house on 18th Avenue and Buchanan was cozy and comfortable compared to the tents, mud huts, and frame houses we had lived in since 1906.

[13.] According to Jennie's 1929 journal, they had 159 visits or contacts with people during the month of April alone. A great many of these people stayed overnight. The house on Buchanan Street had a large bedroom at the front of the house where Robert and Jennie slept, one large and one very small bedroom at the back of the house. There was also a garage where guests were sometimes housed. In the summer, beds were set up outside in the yard to escape the heat.

A trip to downtown Phoenix to the doctor's office, shopping, or movies was a matter of a few minutes by car or by the trolley on Washington Street. The Capitol building was just a few blocks away, and we enjoyed many pleasant hours walking around the beautiful grounds.

I found time to sew for my family and make quilts or curtains for the house. Robert and I planted lots of trees and flowers on our property. We had breadfruit, elm, and tamarisk trees, hedges of pomegranate and oleander, and plenty of vines on trellises to shade the sides of the house. One of the greatest joys of our life was waiting for the poppies and African daisies to pop up each spring in our rock and cactus garden in the back yard.

My father William eventually remarried in California to a widow lady by the name of Ollie Viola Lemon Gorman Hoopengarner. He died on June 27, 1927. Those of the family that were still living gathered at the home of my brother William in Belvedere, California, at 1616 Keenan Street.

William and his new wife, Ollie viola Lemon Gorman Hoopengarner (Photo courtesy Mabel Holmes Stierwalt.)

Our lives were mostly filled with the ordinary happenings of a normal family, and there were some bad times mixed with the good times. For instance, we ended the year 1928 with a series of illnesses. Mary had tonsillitis; Mabel had a severe cold; Bobbie, Billie, Pinkie and I all had the flu. Bobbie had it worse than the rest of us and missed 16 days of school before he got over it entirely. Pinkie's flu turned into an ear infection, and he missed two weeks of school besides the nine days he missed with the flu.

<u>Excerpt from Jennie's personal journal</u>
April 20, 1929

"Wash day today. We got up fairly early. I was nervous when I got up but as the day wore on, I got better. Bobbie helped me do the washing. Sis cleaned up the house. Mabel went to school. I was tired when noon came. Robert went downtown this afternoon. The Bunger boy came and got his radio Bobbie made for him for $3.00. Bobbie, Pinkie, Walter Varner, John and Steve Midzor were planning on a fishing picnic tomorrow. Robert and I went downtown tonight to get something for their lunches. It was crowded on the streets. The new courthouse is finished now and looms up like a castle. Sister went to a council meeting. Chuck said his mother was sick and they had to bring her up from Buckeye to a doctor. Jewel came up this afternoon to see Mabel. Pinkie has been hauling wood all week and Robert gave him a quarter. I got my plates today and they surely are pretty. I got them with 60 Hill coupons."

Trolley cars on Washington Street.
(Photo courtesy Central Arizona Historical Society.)

Keeping us warm in the wintertime was quite a job for Robert. It took a lot of wood to keep us warm and cozy. At least once a week he would go to the outskirts of town to cut firewood for our fireplace and for the wood stove in the kitchen. Sometimes he would take one of the boys to help him, or I would go with him. It was awfully hard getting up on those cold winter mornings. Someone had to get up and get a fire started, and of course, no one wanted to be the one to get out of bed first.

I usually did the laundry on Saturdays so someone in the family would be around to help me. It was a major chore to do the week's laundry, as water had to be heated on the wood stove and carried to the back yard where I had my washing machine. Then the clothes had to be carried to the clotheslines and hung to dry. After everything was washed, the tubs of water were emptied. The clothes were brought in and sorted and put away when they were dry.

Billie 1935

<u>Excerpt from Jennie's personal journal</u>
August 26, 1937
"...Billie cut a door in the back room. I'm going to make a washroom in one end of the bedroom..."

August 27, 1937
"...Had a hard day. Billie and I fixed our washroom today. Made a partition and put in a screen door. Tired tonight. Mabel and kiddies came this afternoon. Bob was here awhile. Robert and I walked around town awhile tonight to cool off. It is so hot in the house--Don't know how we are going to sleep. Everything is dust an inch deep again."

I kept busy sewing, gardening, and keeping house for the family.

Keeping house could get a little complicated on occasions. For instance, in 1929 we had extra boarders, as Sinda and George Henry's 14-year-old son Willard stayed with us for awhile so he could attend high school in Phoenix. George Henry was a brother to Robert's first wife, Alice Henry. George's wife's name was Lucinda and my kids always called her "Aunt Cindy," but I have always known her as "Sinda." The Henrys lived in Buckeye. During that year we also had Uncle Andy, my sister Mary's husband, boarding with us while he worked at the Arizona Light and Power Company. We managed to make room for everyone even though our house only had three bedrooms.

A quilt made by Jennie when Wyona was born.

I did a lot of canning and cooking to keep up with the appetites of my growing family. I made many quilts, both for family and others. I often did sewing for other people to make a little extra money.

<u>Excerpt from Jennie's personal journal</u>
January 21, 1938
"Another beautiful sunny day—just like a spring day—unlike a year ago today. I cleaned house this morning—hung curtains and blinds. Went to the store. This afternoon Mabel came over and we went down to Mrs. Ritter's awhile. She gave me some oleanders for a hedge, also some pomegranate cuttings. Billie will plant them tomorrow. He went to a show tonight. Robert didn't go to work this afternoon. He went to bed. His cold doesn't get any better. It is clear and cold tonight but not cold enough for a fire in the fireplace."

When we moved to Phoenix, I enrolled Bobbie and Pinkie in Jackson School. Pinkie's first grade teacher at St. Johns School,

Mrs. Roberts, had advanced him to doing third grade work before we left there, but when I tried to enroll him in the third grade at Jackson School they wouldn't allow it because he was only six years old. So, Pinkie was placed in the first grade again, and he had a pretty easy time in school for the next couple of years.

Mabel and Mary were enrolled at Adams School (later renamed Grace Court School), as Jackson School only went to the sixth grade. All five of the children eventually graduated from Adams School and went on to Phoenix Union High School.

Excerpt from Jennie's personal journal
Mabel
1st Grade: Mrs. Turney (1916)
2nd and 3rd Grades: Miss Katie Wager

Mary
1st Grade: Miss Katie Wager (1918)

Bobbie
1st Grade: Miss Grumbles (1920)
2nd Grade: Mr. Brightwell
3rd Grade: Mrs. Roberts/Miss Trusdale
4th, 5th, and 6th Grades: Mrs. Goff

Pinkie
1st Grade: Mrs Roberts (1922)

Billie
1st Grade: Miss Mauzy/Miss Baptist (1927)
2nd Grade: Miss Holton

There were many activities for the children to participate in, either through the schools or on their own time. They went to high school basketball games, banquets, plays, track meets, and music festivals, to name a few. The Masque of the Yellow Moon, the big high school pageant put on by Phoenix Union High School, was the highlight of the school year. This pageant eventually involved 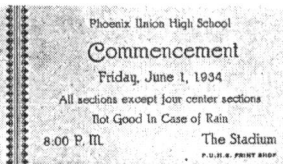 all the high schools in the Phoenix area. Granddaughters, Wyona and Roberta participated in it as students of West Phoenix High School in the 50's. It was held at Montgomery Stadium, and everybody looked forward to this big production every year.

Phoenix Union High School

Sometimes the boys played on basketball teams for the YMCA, attended baseball games at University Park, and went skating, swimming, fishing, picnicking or hunting. The girls taught Sunday school, went for rides, read books, and participated in extracurricular activities at school. The whole family went to parades, wrestling matches, prizefights, picnics, movies at the Orpheum and Rialto theaters. We also watched airplane stunts at the airport, attended the opera (saw "Carmen" in 1929) and attended the State Fair.

Excerpt from Jennie's personal journal
May 31, 1929
"This has been a day of all days...a day I'll never forget— Sister's graduation day...We went to the graduation exercise tonight. There were 407 graduates. They all looked so nice. Chuck took Sister (Charles Olvey and Mary eventually got married). Sister wore a crepe de chine. Mrs. Olvey gave Sis a string of brilliants for graduation. Chuck gave her a Kodak. Mabel gave her a neckless(sic). Jewel gave her a bottle of perfume..."

One of the favorite family activities was traveling all over the state. The roads weren't too good, but that didn't stop us from seeing as much of Arizona as we possibly could. Sometimes Robert had to go to other parts of the state in connection with his job with the Real Estate Board. When it was possible, I would go with him and we would have a little vacation along with business. In 1929 we went on a business trip to the Tucson area, then on down to Tombstone and Bisbee. When we went on a business trip to the Globe area we went to visit some of our family that lived there.

Home from a vacation about 1935.
(Photo courtesy of
William Henry Holmes.)

Vacations to Prescott usually found us staying at Pine Lawn Court. We also stayed there when passing through Prescott on our way to other parts of the state. The White Mountains of northeastern Arizona and Mormon Lake near Flagstaff were also favorite vacation spots.

MORMON LAKE VACATION – AUGUST 1929

Our vacation in August of 1929 was surely one to remember. Robert made arrangements for us to stay in a cabin at Pilgrim's Playground, a church camp at Mormon Lake near Flagstaff. (We stayed there three years in a row.) We planned to stay from August 3 to August 29. We were all very excited about the prospect of going to the cool mountains. We arranged for Sis and Mabel to ride up with Helen Cleveland, as there was no room in our car for all five of us, plus our luggage and groceries, too. We left at 5:45 a.m. and Helen came for the girls about an hour later. Robert, the boys and I got to Prescott at 10:30 a.m. where we visited

Illustration by Eileen Conn, 2017

with Sinda for a few minutes. We continued on to Williams then to Flagstaff, arriving there at 4:00 in the afternoon. We finally got to Pilgrim's Playground at 5:30 p.m. Our cabin was rustic but cozy and comfortable.

In spite of the fact that it was rainy and cool off and on during our stay, there were many nice days in which we went fishing, hiking, and boating. Bobbie, Pinkie, and Billie, being normally curious boys, found many interesting things to do. Once, they found a raft on Lake Mary and the three of them climbed on and floated around, no doubt pretending to be Tom Sawyer and Huckleberry Finn. Another time, they found a handcar on the railroad track and decided to ride it down the track near the cabin. On the way, Pinkie fell off and hit his head. After that, the boys thought they had better do something a little less dangerous, so they occupied their time trying to catch chipmunks.

On August 8 we took a side trip to Sunset Crater north of Flagstaff. It took us an hour to climb to the top of the crater, but it only took five minutes to run down. Billie fell and skinned his face on the way down. We also explored the ice cave near Sunset Crater. The next day we went to Stoneman Lake with the Hudsons, friends who were also staying at Pilgrim's Playground. It was a beautiful drive through the pine trees and aspens, and there were lots of wildflowers blooming everywhere. While we were fishing on the lake in a boat, it started to rain, and we were soaked to the skin before we got back to shore.

August 13 was Bobbie's 15th birthday, and a fishing trip to Marshall Lake made it a special day for him. Bobbie and Pinkie made a raft, and while they were building it, Bobbie ran a nail in his foot. It started to swell up, so I bathed it in turpentine to keep it from getting infected. In spite of the injury Bobbie, Pinkie, and Billie went fishing out on the lake on the raft. They caught so many sunfish that the raft began to sink before they got back to shore!

One day Bobbie, Pinkie, Sister, Mabel, and I decided to hike up Mormon Mountain near the camp. It was a tough climb, but we managed to get to the top. On the way down, it began to storm, and the rain began to pour. We all got soaking wet before we got back to the nice, dry cabin. The next day it continued to rain and hail for two and a half hours until the water was running down the hills in torrents. After the storm was over, Bobbie climbed on the roof of the cabin (no one knows just why he needed to do that) and fell off. But he didn't get hurt, and to prove he was okay, he was out treeing a raccoon the next day.

Illustration by Eileen Conn. 2017

On August 19 we drove to Flagstaff for groceries. From there we visited the Indian ruins at Walnut Canyon. We later took another trip to Marshall Lake and caught 114 fish by 9:30 a.m. There were so many fish we had to give a lot of them away. I cooked some for dinner, but by now I was so sick of fish I didn't care if I ever saw another one! As the dirty clothes piled up, the girls and I brought out the trusty washboard and scrubbed away.

We managed to get the clothes clean in spite of the intermittent rainstorms.

When it rained, we stayed inside and played cards or read books and magazines. But, when the weather permitted, in the evenings all of us went out to the center of the camp and sat around the bonfire to visit with other people in the camp. Sometimes we could hear singing coming from the church, and I enjoyed hearing all those good old church songs. Occasionally, Robert played horseshoes with the other men.

August 29 came all too soon and it was time to go home. We hated to go, but at the same time we were anxious to get back to our daily routines and to see all our pets. We stopped in Prescott

Mary, Jennie, Billie and Mabel showing off the big mess of fish caught at Marshall Lake.
(Photo courtesy of Mary Holmes Olvey.)

on our way home to visit Sinda again. She had just lost a baby and wasn't feeling too well. We stayed overnight at Pine Lawn Court so we could get an early start in the morning. Robert had to get a flat tire fixed and also replaced the battery in the car before leaving Prescott. That wasn't the end of our troubles with the car as we had two more flat tires on the way home. Robert and the boys had quite a time changing those tires in the middle of the hot desert! Even though we had left Prescott at 9:30 a.m., we didn't get home till 3:30 in the afternoon. Home never looked so good! Our pets were glad to see us, too. Our dog, Jinks, climbed in the car and nearly ate us up! The kids scattered to say hello to friends and neighbors, but all I wanted to do was try to rest and cool off.

The vacations and the children's school days were wonderful times of togetherness, but the nest would soon begin to empty. Mabel, Bob and Bill stayed close by in the Phoenix area, but Mary went to far-away Venezuela, South America, to be a missionary. Pinkie moved to California when he got married to Merle. Even though it was hard to let go of our children to begin lives of their own, we kept in touch with family gatherings on holidays and weekends. Those that lived in town would drop by often during the week and have lunch or dinner, or maybe just to say "hello."

When the grandchildren began to come on the scene, Robert and I had a whole new dimension to our lives. It was like starting all over again. I could once again make frilly dresses for little girls, and Robert could take the little ones on his knee and tell them stories and teach them the alphabet from the newspaper headlines. He was also something of an artist and taught Wyona to draw cartoons which she still does today.

CHAPTER 6

Jennie the Mother
--The Empty Nest--

Mabel Belle Holmes

On April 8, 1930, Mabel married Roy Stierwalt, whose family lived two doors down from us on Buchanan Street. Some years after they were married, they bought a little house in Phoenix on 20th Avenue, about one block north of Van Buren. This is where they raised their three girls, Madeline, Mary Belle, and Margaret.

Mabel and Roy Stierwalt celebrated their 50th Wedding Anniversary on April 8th 1980. (Photo courtesy of Mary Belle Stierwalt Garner.)

<u>Excerpt from Jennie's personal journal</u>
January 1, 1931
Another year for the Holmes family—1931. Last year was a very short one with haps and mishaps of which I didn't keep track of after Mabel got married. We didn't go away last summer to the mountains. We painted the kitchen and bedroom instead. Robert and I took a few trips in different parts of the state.

Robert, Bobbie, Pinkie and Willard went to the lake and Canyon for a week. Mabel stayed with us all summer till October, then R. V. (Johnson) gave Roy work and they moved to themselves out on East Pierce. Roy is out of work again so I don't know how long they will be there. Chuck went to Colorado this summer so Sis spent a very lonely summer.

"I was on the election board again in November—got $18. Robert and I went to Kingman in October. We went through snow in Ashfork. Mary (Jennie's sister) came out in May, and she and Andy got a divorce. She is married again. We had a nice Christmas. We all got lots of presents...Bobbie took the 'Republican' route and Pinkie the 'Gazette'."

(Author note-the <u>Arizona Republic</u> and <u>Phoenix Gazette</u> were the newspapers for the Phoenix area.)

In 1938, Roy went to work for the post office and worked there until he retired. After her three girls were all in school, Mabel got a degree in education at Arizona State College (now Arizona State University). She taught at Cashion School and retired after teaching for about 20 years. She learned to speak Spanish fluently so as to be able to communicate with her little Spanish-speaking students. The school at Cashion was not far from the ranch where we lived before we moved to Phoenix in 1923.

Mabel and Roy with Mary Belle, Margaret and Madeline at their home on 20th Avenue.

Chuck and Mary Olvey. (Photo courtesy of Violet Hopkins Holmes.)

Mary Alice Holmes

Mary got acquainted with a boy named Charles "Chuck" Olvey who delivered the Phoenix Gazette newspaper to our house. They were both active in R. V. Johnson's church, and this is where they fell in love. Mary and Chuck were married on May 15, 1932, and soon afterward decided to become missionaries. They attended Biola Institute in Los Angeles (now Biola University) for four years. In October 1937, they left for Venezuela, South America, where they spent 42 years with the Orinoco River Mission. They went to the University of Oklahoma at Norman in 1942 when they were on their first furlough to learn how to interpret an unwritten language to writing. This was a concentrated course in linguistic training. They learned how to translate the Panare and the Maquiretare languages as these were the main tribes they worked with while in Venezuela.

When Mary and Chuck left to go so far away, I thought the world was coming to an end, and I was sure that I would never get over it. Robert was a great help to me during this trying time by encouraging me to look at it as something that had to be, and it was what they really wanted to do. With Robert's help, I finally learned to accept it and was glad they were able to do something so important.

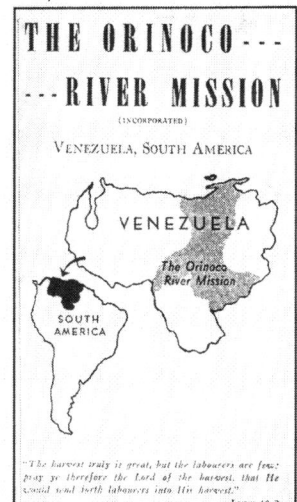

Excerpt from Jennie's personal journal
October 24, 1937

"...We all got ready and went over to Sister's church...We went to the dining room for dinner. They gave us quite a reception and send off. Uncle Bill and Ophie and her mother were there to go to the boat with us. Roy Bancroft ate dinner with us and he and Winona went with Uncle Bill in his car, Sister with us, and Chuck went with his uncle. We all got to the boat at 3:30 p.m. What a boat! (S.S. California.) We went all over it. There was a big crowd to see the kids (Mary and Chuck) off. They have a nice little stateroom. We all went out to the café for supper. Roy and Winona ate with us, then we went back to the boat for a few minutes then bade the kids goodbye. I hated to leave my darling girl but had to...Little Jimmie had a good time on the boat, also Billie got a kick out of it all."

Lynn on her first birthday. Dec 8, 1948. (Photo courtesy of William H. Holmes.)

Mary and Chuck didn't have any children of their own, but they unofficially adopted two girls while they were missionaries in South America. Salma Souki was born in Venezuela and eventually married Albert Gusiff and went to live in Whittier, California. Evelyn (Lynn) Prussell was born in Washington, D.C. and was the child of Chuck's mother's oldest brother. Lynn's mother died in childbirth, and her father asked Chuck and Mary to raise Lynn for him. Lynn married a man named Pierno Salerno from Venezuela and is still living there with her husband and six children. Even though Salma and Lynn were not legally adopted, they always considered Chuck and Mary their parents.

Salma

Robert Ullock Holmes

Bobbie graduated from Phoenix Union High School in 1932 and shortly afterward went into the Civilian Conservation Corps (CCC) where he helped make camping areas and trails in many national parks in Colorado and Arizona. In June 1936 he married Violet Christine Hopkins and they had ten children spaced over a 25-year period.

Robert Ullock Homes age 16.

Excerpt from Jennie's personal journal
June 20, 1936

"Bob and Violet got married. Sister was here. We walked up to the Capitol church. They were married at 5:30 in the preacher's home just behind the church. Rev. Cook married them. Papa was working in Casa Grande at the time, but came home too late for the wedding that day..."

After Bob settled down and got married, he became an electrician, and from November 7, 1937 to September 12, 1938 he worked on the construction of Bartlett Dam on the Verde River. In March 1938 there were heavy rains all over the state, and the river came down in a torrent and washed away their tent. Vi and Wyona came to live with us for awhile. After the flooding receded, they moved back to the dam on March 29. Wyona learned to walk

Bartlett Dam about 1938.

during the time they lived at the dam, and Vi almost died from a scorpion sting. So things were primitive and sometimes scary during that time.

Excerpt from Jennie's personal journal
March 3, 1938
"What a day! It has been raining all day. About 4:30 there came a wind and rain pouring down like water out of a bucket... Bob and Vi came in about 9:30 tonight all tired out from the long drive down (from Bartlett Dam). It had been raining for five days up there and had driven them to higher ground but all their bedding was wet...We haven't heard a word from Pinkie, and L.A. (Los Angeles) is all under water with floods, death and destruction. We are so worried and anxious about him. The Salt River is up from bank to bank and still rising..." (Author's note: The Verde and Salt Rivers come together near Phoenix and the heavy rains were impacting all the rivers during this time.)

When Bob left the dam, he worked for different people doing wiring. Then in 1941 he started to work for DeBerge and Babcock Electric, located at 5th Avenue and Washington in Phoenix. In 1946 he bought into the business and was a partner, at which time the name was changed to DeBerge and Holmes Electric and was at times considered the second largest electrical contracting company in Arizona.

Bob and Vi holding Wyona 1937.

Bob and Vi loved the outdoors and passed this love on to all ten of their children. They took them on many camping and fishing trips around the state of Arizona long before there were good roads to get to the fishing holes. Their favorite camping places were the White Mountains and the Mogollon Rim. They also spent many summers vacationing in Prescott where they rented a cabin at the Hideaway Court.

In 1939 they bought a little stucco house in west Phoenix on 31st Avenue south of Buckeye Road. Soon, Bob expanded the little house adding on a large living room and an extra bedroom for Mary and Bobby. In time, even this wasn't enough room for all the kids, so in 1952 the family moved to north Phoenix on 23rd Avenue and Campbell. Eventually, this house was added onto but they still made another move to 32nd Street and Mariposa in east Phoenix to a house with six bedrooms. The last house they lived in that they owned was off of 16th Street and Northern on Winter Drive. As the family evolved with the children going out on their own, there were many more moves along the way, too many to count.

The Bob Holmes Clan. Top row from left: Kevin, Bob Jr., John, Ed. Middle Row: Melinda (Suzie) Garrido, Roberta Adams: Bottom Row: Mary McKnight, Nancy Holmes, Wyona Jaffe. Gary is absent from photo. (Photo by Irving Jaffe March 1986).

James Wilson Holmes

James Wilson Holmes about 1936. (Photo courtesy of William H. Holmes.)

Pinkie had a bad time health wise all his life. When he was in the eighth grade he had smallpox. We don't know where he got it, as none of the other kids at school had it. While he was confined with the smallpox, Robert, Bobbie and Billie slept in the garage so they wouldn't get it. In spite of his prolonged absence, he went on to graduate with his class. During his freshman year in high school he fell and ruptured his appendix and had to have an operation. He had the operation on May 21 and came home from the hospital on June 3. He missed the end of that school year but managed to make it up so he could graduate with the rest of his class in 1934.

Excerpt from Jennie's personal journal
    Christmas 1937
    "This has been a wonderful Christmas. We got up at 7:30. I made the fires and got breakfast. Billie got up. He opened his presents. Robert got up. I got Wyona up and dressed her. Vi got up. We started to eat. Bob got up and here come Pinkie and Merle. We finished our breakfast and did we have a joyous time opening our gifts. We all got plenty such nice useful presents. Chi sent us all something. After breakfast Robert went after Mabel and Roy. The kiddies were just loaded with toys. Wyona and Jimmie had a time with dolls and wind-ups..."

James Wellington with daughter.

Pinkie married Merle Gibbons in 1935, moved to Los Angeles, and went to work for Pacific Freight Lines as a truck driver. He was soon elected business agent of their local union. Pinkie and Merle had one son, James Wellington, born December 15, 1936. Pinkie divorced Merle and later married Margaret (Peggy) Walsh in 1940. He developed leukemia and returned to Phoenix where he worked for DeBerge and Babcock Electric until he was too ill to work. He died in 1943 at the young age of 26.

The three Holmes Boys: Bob, Pinkie, Billie. August 1942. (Photo courtesy of William H. Holmes.)

William Henry Holmes

William Henry Holmes and his bride, Bernice Brogdon shortly after their wedding Oct 18, 1947. (Photo courtesy of Violet Holmes.)

Bill graduated from Phoenix Union High School in 1939, the largest class ever up till that time—1280 plus. Phoenix was growing in those years and North Phoenix High School opened the following year. Bill worked for a while with Bob at DeBerge and Holmes Electric. When there wasn't any work available, his dad got him a job with the Maricopa County Highway Department as a laborer. In November 1940 he went to work for New State Electric and worked on Luke Air Force Base, Williams Field, Ajo, Gila Bend, and Marana Airfields.

Excerpt from Jennie's personal journal
June 4, 1937
"...Robert painted the table Billie made at school. Looks nice. Will get the chest of drawers (from school) tomorrow. I'm going to put it in Bob's room for Vi to put their clothes in, then someday Billie will put his in it. It is his when he has a place of his own. Billie painted his Ford today. It looks real cute..."

Bill joined the army on October 7, 1942, and took basic training at Camp Callan about four miles north of LaJolla California. He went overseas in February of 1943 and went directly to Africa where he was assigned to radars. From Africa he went to Italy and wound up on the border of Switzerland at the end of the campaign. In July of 1945 he was shipped from Leghorn, Italy, through the canal, across the Pacific to Manila. His company landed on the day the armistice was signed, so they just waited for a ride home. He arrived in the United States in San Pedro, California, on Thanksgiving Day 1945 and was discharged two days later.

He went to work in January 1946 for DeBerge and Holmes Electric, where he worked until May 1967. After that he worked for Howard Electric till June 1982. His next job was with Bechtel Corporation at the Palo Verde Nuclear plant near Buckeye. He then retired in December 1982.

Bill met Bernice "Bernie" Brogdon in the summer of 1939 on a vacant lot near her Grandmother Ralston's home on 17th Avenue and Buchanan at a neighborhood baseball game. On their first date, Bill walked Bernie home from a neighbor's birthday party. They were engaged in the summer of 1941 and married on October 18, 1947, in a wedding chapel in Phoenix. Their first home was at 2538 West Jefferson, where they lived for eight years. They have three girls, Zoe Ann, Zona Lee, and Zena Rae. They moved to 3817 West Earll Drive, where they still live today. (Author's note: This was referring to 1978.)

Bill in his Army uniform- Italy, July 4, 1944. (Photo courtesy of William H. Holmes.)

CHAPTER 7

Jennie the Grandmother

Robert and Jennie on their 35th wedding anniversary November 6, 1941. (Photo courtesy of Mabel Holmes Stierwalt.)

This chapter of Jennie's Journal will be written not by Jennie, but by Jennie's grandchildren and great grandchildren. Since she died in 1978, many of the younger grandchildren have little or no memory of her, but those who do were asked to share some of their special memories.---Wyona Holmes Jaffe

Prickly Pear Cactus

Madeline Stierwalt Wallace

Growing up with grandparents is special!!! My sisters and I were extra blessed with having both sets of grandparents living nearby during our childhood years. In order to distinguish them by name, we called one grandmother "Big Mom" and Jennie Lee was "Little Mom." She was little in stature, but big-hearted, strong, and full of love and caring for her family and friends. I will always remember the warmth and acceptance in Little Mom and Grandpa's home whether we were there for a big holiday dinner, an overnight stay, or just stopping by after school with friends.

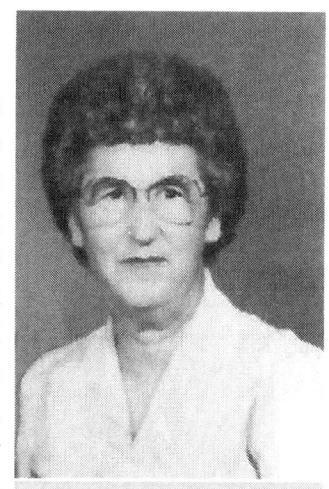

Madeline Stierwalt Wallace. 1987 (Photo courtesy of Madeline Stierwalt.)

When I was to be married, Little Mom wrote to me, "I don't know why you have to go clear East to Kansas to marry and live. It is so far from home." The long train ride from Denver to Wichita almost made me have second thoughts about the whole thing, too. Her advice on marriage was, "If you want to have a happy marriage, it's entirely up to you." I often think of this when I veer too far toward being a "liberated woman."

Children were very important to Little Mom. She always knew the names of each new child in the family and loved showing you their pictures. Our last trip to see Little Mom was the Christmas just before she died. Diana, our daughter, stayed nights with her and still remembers how the beds were covered with gifts to all the little children. Each one was special to her.

All through the night Diana heard Little Mom sob softly. Was it because she was so lonely, knew this might be her last Christmas, or was she thankful that she had been a part in establishing roots for so many of us?

Excerpt from Jennie's personal journal
February 26, 1938
"...Madeline baked my birthday cake—a nice big one with coconut on it. We ate part of it for supper tonight. It was so good..."

Mary Belle Stierwalt Garner

I remember "Little Mom" that's what Madeline, Margaret and I always called her. She lived two houses from our other grandmother who was bigger and she was "Big Mom." That's how we told them apart. Little Mom always had a yard full of chickens. We would go over every Sunday and Grandpa would chop off the chicken's head, and then Little Mom did the rest. We helped pluck the thing and then had chicken and dumplings. I wouldn't eat chicken for years and still won't unless in the mood. Little Mom was quite a cook on her wood stove. I don't remember the year she got the electric one, but I know she still liked the wood one for a lot of things. She was a very good cook. I always try to get my red beans and ham to turn out thick like hers but never made it. Maybe it was the wood stove.

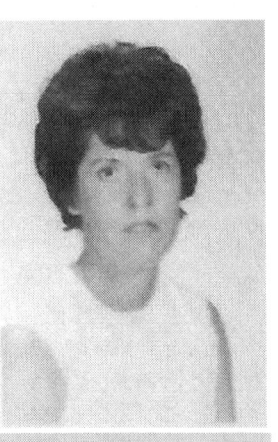

Mary Belle Stierwalt Garner. (Photo courtesy of Mary Belle Stierwalt Garner.)

We used to help her churn butter and then drink the buttermilk. Little Mom was very

Robert with his arms full of grandchildren: Mary Belle, Madeline, Roberta and Wyona. (Photo courtesy of William H. Holmes.)

family-oriented. Her house was open to any relative regardless of how distant. If they came to town, she would be very hurt if they didn't stay there or at least come by for a while. She and her neighbor friends always had a quilt frame set up working on a quilt. After Grandpa passed away, she moved next door to my folks and did her own housework. The place was very neat and clean. She kept every card she was ever sent and could tell you when and who sent it. Her family was her pride and joy.

Excerpt from Jennie's personal journal
December 10, 1937
"Mary Bell is four years old today. I made her two hankies and Billie gave her two. She wanted eight! Mabel made her a nice cake..."
September 19, 1938
"Mabel and kiddies came over this afternoon. Mary Belle started to school today. She doesn't know whether she likes it or not..."

Margaret Stierwalt Beatty

These are some of the memories I have of Little Mom. She taught me how to sew on her treadle machine and how to crochet. I remember her excitement when Uncle Bob got her an electric stove to replace the wood stove. I thought her wood stove was fun! Little Mom would have chicken and dumpling dinners on Sundays. She always had a great pride in her cactus garden.

The things I remember most about Grandpa are his rocking chair, reading us stories, and the beautiful books he gave us every Christmas. I remember him working in his little workshop making cactus picture

Margaret Stierwalt Beatty. (Photo courtesy of Mary Belle Garner.)

frames and lamps. One time he got really angry with Little Mom when she cleaned his pipe tobacco humidor in Clorox! Oh! Was he mad! He told us stories about how he lost his finger, how he played the fiddle at dances, how he came to America, and about his days as a sheriff. He was my favorite Grandpa.

Robert in his comfortable old rocking chair. (Photo courtesy of Mary Holmes Olvey.)

Grandpa's cactus lamps.

Wyona Holmes Jaffe 1980

Wyona Holmes Jaffe

One of my most vivid memories of Grandma's house was watching the trains that passed in back of the house. My brothers and sisters and I would run to the back fence when we heard the whistle of an oncoming train. The trains always whistled because they crossed over 18th and 19th Avenues just west of Grandma's house. The engineers would wave at those four little kids, and we were thrilled to think someone as wonderful as an engineer would take the time to pay attention to us.

Roberta, Bobby, Wyona and Mary waving at the Engineer.
Pen and Ink sketch by Bob Eckel.

I have nine brothers and sisters but only four of us clearly remember the time Grandma and Grandpa lived on Buchanan Street. After Grandpa died in 1963, Grandma moved to 20th Avenue next to Mabel and Roy.

When we were small my sisters, Roberta, and Mary and I loved to go to Grandma's house so we could play house on the front porch. It was enclosed by a brick wall about three feet high, just high enough to give us the feeling that we had a real "house" to have tea with our dolls. Grandma supplied us with plenty of homemade cookies and "tea" to make the occasion special.

The fireplace with the chiming clock on the mantel was a familiar sight, and I never think of Grandma's house without seeing that fireplace in my mind's eye. When I was about five years old, Grandpa took me on his knee and taught me the alphabet from the headlines in the newspapers. He also taught me to draw funny little cartoon characters. (I still draw funny little cartoon characters!)

Excerpt from Jennie's personal journal
January 27, 1937
"This has been some day. I was awakened this a.m. about 2:00 by Bob. Vi was sick. I got up and in a half hour we had her ready to go to the hospital. (Vi was expecting their first baby, Wyona.) We borrowed Bud's car as ours was out of order, of course, at a time like this. Bob drove and I held Vi on my lap and I must have been sitting on tire pumps and a jack or whatever as I was nearly dead by the time we got to the hospital. The baby girl was born at 4:45. She weighed 5 lbs., black hair and head just like Bob's. Both Vi and baby are fine..."

Grandma had trouble with my name at first (most people do) and called me "Wynona May" after I was born. By February 11 (in her journals) I was "Wyonia." By February 13 she got it right "Wyona."

On the holidays, while the family was still small enough to gather around the table, we would have the family gatherings at Grandma and Grandpa's house. The grown-ups ate at the big table in the dining room and all the children ate at the kitchen table. I remember what a thrill it was to finally be "big" enough to eat at the table with the adults. These family gatherings were always happy times for us.

On Easter, we hunted Easter eggs in the yard as there were so many places to hide them around the trees and bushes. At Christmas time, when Uncle Chuck and Aunt Mary were home on furlough from South America (which was every five years), we strung a piñata on a rope between the breadfruit tree and the Elm tree in the front yard. All of us kids took a turn at being blindfolded and taking swings at the piñata. If someone connected with a good healthy swing, we got to pick up candies and goodies that burst out of the piñata.

Easter at Grandma and Grandpa's about 1947 taken in front of Grandma's cactus and flower garden in the back yard. Left to right: Margaret, Mary Belle, Roberta, Bobby, Wyona, Madeline, Mary.

On New Year's Day our tradition was to go on a picnic somewhere on the desert. Grandpa made frames and lamps from cactus wood, and we made it a time of looking for wood and enjoying the desert. Some of us have continued this tradition of a desert outing on New Year's Day. In later years, when the family had gotten too large to gather at Grandma's house, we went on picnics for Easter and Thanksgiving Day. Sometimes we went to South Mountain Park, sometimes to Sycamore Creek near Sugarloaf Mountain or Bloody Basin.

The best thing I remember about my grandparents is that they made me feel <u>special</u>, and I hope my own grandchildren can say that about me someday.

Roberta Holmes Adams

I guess the things I remember about Grandma are the Easter egg hunts in the yard, her flowers, the trains roaring through the back yard in the middle of the night, the noisy clock on the mantel that struck on the hour, and the first Bible verse I ever memorized hanging on the living room wall, John 3:16.

Roberta Holmes Adams. 1987.

I especially remember the year I visited with her every afternoon after school when I was in the 8th grade. We had moved away from Murphy School where I had attended for seven years (from 31st Avenue and Buckeye to 23rd Avenue and Indian School Road in 1951) and I wanted to graduate from there. I took the school bus to Grandma's every day after school and Daddy picked me up there and took me home. Maybe I spent more time with her than most of the grandchildren because of that experience, but I enjoyed just visiting and talking with her. I'm glad I have good memories of my grandmother. Maybe it will make me a better grandmother.

Mary Holmes McKnight

I remember one day when Bobby and I were staying at Grandma's we got into the incinerator out in the back by the fence near the railroad tracks. We took coals and covered ourselves from head to toe with the black coal. Needless to say, Grandma was furious and took us directly to the bathroom and proceeded to scold (and maybe spank?) us at some length while she tried to get the black off!

Mary Holmes McKnight

I remember the big bathtub that sat up off of the floor on those funny little legs, and the old toilet with the tank on the ceiling. And I also remember Grandpa's razor strap hanging on the wall.

Zoe Ann Holmes Ravert

I have many memories of Grandma, and I feel very fortunate to have spent so much time with her, especially in the years of my life when I was learning and appreciating so much.

There were trips at Thanksgiving and Easter where our family, along with many relatives and friends, went out into the desert and had picnics, egg hunts, and rock hunts. Grandma was always teaching us the names of each flower, cactus, or rock. We all learned to appreciate and love the Arizona desert. She loved rocks and flowers and had them all around her house. She taught us to see and hear things: the sunsets, flowers, and birds.

Zoe Ann and Jerry Ravert. 1987. (Photo courtesy of Zoe Ann Ravert.)

Then there were times that Grandma was very fearful of the desert. This was during our summer thunderstorms. She hated them because of an experience she had when she was a small girl on the ranch (in the Verde Valley). One of the horses got struck by lightning and was killed. Grandma never forgot that,

Jennie in her kitchen in the little house at 340 N 20th Drive next door to Mable and Roy. (Photo courtesy of Zoe Ann Ravert.)

and the thunderstorms really upset her.

I stayed with her a lot during the summers after Grandpa died. We did sewing, cooking, and gardening during that time. She made dresses without patterns, and she was always making something for her grandchildren. She made quilts out of old blouses and dresses and crocheted beautifully. She was the kind of cook that took a pinch of this and a handful of that and turned out wonderful apple pies.

I remember Grandma's belief in the Lord. After Grandpa died, she didn't want to stay in a lonely house, so she came to stay with us (Bill, Bernie and three girls) for awhile. I thought it was great because she shared my bedroom. Grandma read her Bible every morning, afternoon, and before going to bed. I only wish we would have shared that time together because I'm sure she would have taught me so much. But when you are a sophomore in high school, you have other things on your mind. That will be one of those things in life I will always regret, now that I'm older.

I also remember a time when Grandma and her brother, Uncle

Jennie and brother, Verde, 'having a little music'. 1954
(Photo courtesy of William H. Holmes.)

Verde, played the guitar and fiddle together. I remember sitting in fascination while they played.

Excerpt from Jennie's personal journal
August 27, 1937
"Nice breeze this a.m. Got up at 3:30. Robert and Billie left for Parker and Yuma at 6 o'clock. I cleaned the house up and then got breakfast. Sis and Chuck got up. Then went in Bob's car to get Frankie (Suddarth). Bob brought his car down for us to go after figs over to Sally's. Mabel and I went and picked them. The bees stung Mabel. I climbed the trees as good as ever. Got about 45 pounds of figs—canned them after dinner. Sis got dinner and kept Frankie for me. I got through at 7:15—tired out...Mable helped fix the figs to cook..."

I will always remember Grandma as a small, sometimes frail woman. But her strength was not in her physical size, but the size of her heart. She taught me to use my heart and feel for people and small creatures. She loved her kittens and cats. She saw beauty in everything, living or nonliving. She loved and cared for her family, being happy when they were happy, and hurting when they hurt. In that way, she was a great influence in my life and will always be remembered.

Zona Lee Holmes Finney

One thing about living so far away, you don't see your family very often. The last time I saw Grandma was in 1974, about two years after my husband and I moved to Illinois. I came back for a short visit. We took Grandma on a picnic at a park. We fed the ducks and had a real nice visit.

I remember when we went on family picnics or get-togethers

Zona Lee, Jennie, and my mom, Bernie (Photo courtesy of Zona Lee Finney.)

in the desert or mountains Grandma would go rock hunting. She came home with all kinds of rocks. Now, when we go on vacations, we go rock hunting, too. She loved her flowers. She grew different kinds and was very proud of them. One of her favorites was her hibiscus bush. It was beautiful.

I love her and miss her very much. But I still hold the hope of the resurrection and one day hope to see her again, and then she will be seeing her great grandchildren for the first time.

Zena Rae Holmes Smith

My most touching memory of Grandma was our last Christmas with her. I was so, so touched when she gave me her silver set that her children gave to her and Grandpa on their 50th wedding anniversary, and she also gave me a crocheted bedspread she made for me. She also gave me a photo album that she told me the first pictures to go in it were to be my wedding pictures. That is what is in it. The <u>whole</u> thing is full of my wedding pictures. I'm only sorry that she is not in any of them.

Zena Rae Holmes Smith 1987. (Photo courtesy of William H. Holmes.)

Photo from the Phoenix Gazette November 1956

50TH ANNIVERSARY

An open house Sunday, Nov. 18 will honor Mr. and Mrs. John R. Holmes, 1746 W. Buchanan, on their 50th wedding anniversary. The couple was married here Nov. 18, 1906. Three of their four children live here, Robert U., William Henry, and Mrs. Roy Stierwalt, 344 N. 20th Dr., in whose home the reception will be held.

Deborah Lynn Reeder

I feel quite honored to have been allowed to work on this book with my mother, Wyona. It has rekindled many fond memories and feelings for Great Grandma Jennie. My only regret is that I didn't spend more time with Grandma before she left us, and was too young to fully appreciate Grandpa before he passed away.

My earliest recollections are of the big old brick house with the trains passing by, and Grandma's old three-legged calico cat, Patches. Later came many other cats, such as Rusty and Cindy. It seems every time I saw her she was holding and loving a cat. Perhaps that is where I inherited by great love for animals. She also instilled in her family a sense of pride and appreciation for people as well as nature that I am grateful was handed down to each generation.

Deborah Lynn Reeder. 1985

Great Grandma also had a very strong sense of "family." She protected her family like a cougar would her cubs. I can even remember her admonishing both Mother and me to be sure not to drag out any family skeletons, should we find any while researching the book, to embarrass anyone. I was touched by her shyness about being the subject of an

Jennie with great-grand daughter, Deborah. 1956.

entire book, too. She was a bit bewildered, I think, about why it was so important to my mother to write this book about her. The special time we spent with her listening to and taping her stories will be what I will remember with the greatest fondness the rest of my life.

Kristi Adams Koerber

I will never forget the sweet memories of going over to visit for a few hours with Grandma Jennie Lee—usually on our way back home to Bullhead City. We would stop by to say Hello! She always greeted us with a beautiful smile and cookies. We went out and sat in her nice little front yard and enjoyed her pretty flowers. She always was such a happy soul and looked so pretty in her dresses that she wore. It would be so nice to have a hug from her and to see her smile. Miss you, Grandma Jennie Lee!

Kristi Adams Koerber. (Photo courtesy of Roberta Adams.)

Appendix

Wyona at one of her favorite places-Heart Prairie near Flagstaff, Arizona. (Photo by Deborah Reeder).

APPENDIX #1
Murder of Williamson Hawkins

The following story is about the unfortunate demise of Williamson Hawkins, father of William Henry Hawkins, Sr. (William was adopted by Williamson and his wife, Rebecca. There is no record of how the adoption came about or anything about William's birth parents.) Williamson was born in 1795 in Henry County, Tennessee, and died in September 1838 in Blue Springs, Jackson County, Missouri.

Murder of Williamson Hawkins: 10 May 1839
This tragic-comedy episode results in the first legal hanging in Jackson County, Missouri.

In 1833, Williamson Hawkins bought land on the "Little Blue" River to build a sawmill, and in one way or another, became very prosperous. He also had a wife whom he was very fond of ---"beating" that is. She did not share his enthusiasm for this pastime.

The fond couple found time between chastisements to have a number of children, but Rebecca Hawkins, the recipient of these endearments, rather resented the regular thumping bestowed upon her by her doting husband. She thought to terminate the affair by using "rat poison" to season Williamson's vittles. However, he was the personification of the Hardy Pioneer, and continued to thrive upon the diet. Rebecca determined to speed up the action and engaged an accomplice from her husband's sawmill, Henry Garster.

Kansas City Times – 2 March 1878 records:
"The murdered man, Hawkins, was a well-to-do miller. His wife became tired of him beating her and after two attempts to poison her husband, hired Garster to shoot him. She stole

$100 from her husband with which to pay the murderer for his brutal act. She than took out a portion of the chinking from between the logs of the house they lived in so her accomplice could shoot her husband from the outside. Hawkins was shot while he sat by the fireplace, the weapon used being an old-fashioned squirrel rifle. Garster was tried and found guilty."

On December 4, 1838, the widow Hawkins and Henry Garster were both indicted for murder by poisoning, the charges on this count were dismissed. Rebecca asked for and received bail, but Henry was remanded to jail. He tunneled out of the old log jailhouse in Independence, but was apprehended in southwest Missouri—a born loser.

Rebecca had "friends"—people with prospects of large inheritances always have friends. Large inheritances mean large administration fees, profitable guardianships, and years of execution. She needed "powerful friends" for the changes of venue, continuances, bail money, and postponements were expensive. She was tried for the "shooting" murder and found guilty. Sentenced to five years in prison, judgment was appealed July 1841. Rebecca never went to jail—the innocent are always protected by Providence. By 1850 Williamson Hawkins' estate was still being administered by his son, Pendleton.

The miscreant, Henry Garster, was given his day in court and was hung on 10 May 1839. He was taken to the town commons in a wagon seated on his coffin driven by Sheriff John King. King had a vested interest in the demise of Garster: a surety bond was issued involving 160 acres of land for the sum of $150 to Garster's defense attorney. Upon Garster's hanging, the land would fall to the contributors. Four days after the hanging, John King appeared before the Jackson County Court with the surety bond to record his deed. It had been recorded the same day it was drawn up.

Vol. X (June 1974) of the West Port Historical Quarterly Compiled by William A. Goff from Jackson County Historical Society Archives, Independence, Missouri.

APPENDIX #2
Military Record of William Henry Hawkins

The following information regarding William Henry Hawkins, Sr. was forwarded to my nephew, Matthew Holmes, while he was researching William's military record:

March 22, 2013
From: Dr. Robert Massey, AZ Division of Research

Mr. Holmes,
I am pleased to confirm that William Henry Hawkins did serve in the army of the Confederate States during the War for Southern Independence. I've found the following:
July 26, 1863 Enlisted (Howell Co. MO) Pvt Co. D, Woods Bat. MO Cavalry
Oct. 25, 1863 Wounded, Mine Creek, KN
Oct. 25, 1863 Captured, Mine Creek KN
(date not given) POW , US Army Post, Mound City, KN
Nov 1, 1863 POW transferred to Post hospital (gun shot wound)
Dec 21, 1863 POW transferred to Ft. Leavenworth, KN
Jan 4, 1865 POW transferred to Post hospital, Ft. Leavenworth, KN
(date not given) POW transferred to US Military Prison, St. Louis
Mar 3, 1865 POW transferred for Exchange to US Military Prison, Alton IL
June 1, 1865 Discharged w/Oath of Allegiance, Alton IL
June 13, 1865 Paroled, Batesville, AK

FYI While researching the service of William H. Hawkins, I discovered that there was another William H. Hawkins serving in "the same unit." Could this be a son of William H. Hawkins Sr. or other relative? The national archives file treated these two soldiers as the same person. The file held aprox 27 entries and they were not filed in order by date. Both soldiers were captured within one day of each other and were transferred around. It was very confusing until I found that they enlisted in different places and different times and were discharged on different dates...both served under Gen. Sterling Price, both were POW's, both captured in Kansas a day apart, both were hospitalized. One is listed as being in Woods Bat. MO Cav., the other is in Co A, 14th MO Cav. Should be easy, except Woods Bat. MO Cav was officially known in the CSA Army as the 14th MO Cav. It would seem that the William H. Hawkins that enlisted in Howell Co. MO would give his unit as Woods...and the William H. Hawkins that enlisted in Arkansas gave his unit as 14th MO Cav. Oh, and just to confuse things...I did a Google search for Howell Co. MO...it is on the border between MO &AR. Here is what I have on the other William H. Hawkins:

July 9, 1864 Enlisted (Pocahontas, AR) pvt. Co A, 14th MO Cavalry

Oct 24, 1864 Captured, Mound City, KN

Nov 3, 1864 POW US Military Prison, Gratiot St., St. Louis, MO

Nov 26, 1864 POW transferred to US Military Prison, Alton, IL

Dec 7, 1864 POW transferred to US Military Prison, Rock Island, IL

Feb 25, 1865 POW transferred for exchange, City Point, VA CSA

Mar 2, 1865 Jackson Hospital, CSA, Richmond, VA

Mar 7, 1865 3rd Division Gen. Hospital CSA, Richmond, VA (CSA Military Hospitals were taken over by US troops in April 1865)

APPENDIX #3
1875: First Families; William and Harriet Hawkins Family
Source: Verde Independent March 13, 2013

By Verde Heritage, Cottonwood, AZ
Heritage and History: Friday, January 25, 2013

"Parson" James Clawson Bristow wrote about traveling from Missouri to Arizona Territory. "Soon after we passed Fort Scott we came upon Hawkins. He had been across the plains in an early day to California. He had something near one hundred cows and some horses. Now we number in all, women and children, about fifty."

They were traveling through New Mexico. "Here we came to two roads that they said would lead us to where we wanted to go, but advised us to take the left hand. Hawkins would not do it. Hawkins seemed to have some knowledge of the country. He had a brother who traveled with a drove of cattle from Texas to Prescott, and I suppose that he got some knowledge of the route from him. So we parted, leaving me and Jim Human, and Hawkins alone. Hawkins was a man that when he set his head to do a thing Uncle Sam could not turn him from the course that he had lined out to go…When in about two miles of Las Vegas, horses were stolen; two from Hawkins and the last horse I had…I do not remember how far it was from Albuquerque to Wingate."

"We reached the Reservation about a mile up the river from the Fort. We did not go to the Fort. There we camped on the night of the 17th, and on the 18th we camped near where the old adobe was built. …In a few days…Cumi and Rastus Hawkins went up to Prescott and were married. Then Hawkins moved up to Peck's Lake."

("A Sketch of the History of My Traveling from Southwest Missouri to Arizona" by James Clawson Bristow; Middle Verde, October 5, 1909; typed manuscript; pages 3, 5, 8; from Sedona Heritage Museum.)

"Parson" James Clawson and Luranda C. (Smith) Bristow traveled to Arizona Territory with 6 of their children, which included Mary (b. 11-09-1857) and her husband, James W. Human, who were married January 31, 1875. Another daughter, Talitha Cumi Bristow (b. 09-03-1861) married David Erastus Hawkins.

William Henry Hawkins and Harriet Melissa Strayton were married on January 23, 1852 in Independence, Missouri. Later, they took their family to California. William (b. 02-07-1855, in Stockton) and James (b. 01-28-1861) and their other children returned to Missouri. The Hawkins family came to Arizona in 1875 with 9 children, arriving in the Verde Valley with the "Parson" Bristow family.

Morris A. Ruffner, credited with the discovery of what became the United Verde mine, was "living near the vicinity of Peck's Lake when the first wagon train of pioneers came into the district." Morris Ruffner, who had been a Confederate soldier, sold his ranch to William Hawkins, who also had been a Confederate soldier. The Hawkins family settled there and Morris Ruffner lived near them or with them "while investigating the mineral possibilities of the surrounding country." (Verde Copper News; September 28, 1928; page 1, column 6.)

COTTONWOOD CEMETERY BURIALS OF THE HAWKINS FAMILY (Partial list)

JOHN HAWKINS: Son of William and Harriet Hawkins,

was the first person buried in what became the Cottonwood Cemetery.

SARA E. HAWKINS ALDERSON (b. 12-25-1854, Independence, MO) is buried near her brother. She died January 26, 1879. "Sad Accident...Mrs. Sara Alderson, of Upper Verde or Peck's Lake, about the 18th inst., while standing near a fire, had the misfortune to have her clothes take fire and nearly all burned from her person. Her husband discovered her situation and in an instant came to her rescue, but was unable to extinguish the flames, as there was no water in the house, at the time. He was compelled to carry his wife to a small lake of water adjacent to their dwelling before he was able to extinguish the fire. Mrs. Alderson was badly burned, and died from the effects of her injuries on Sunday night last. We sympathize with Mr. Alderson in his misfortune, which took from him a devoted wife, and with Mr. and Mrs. Hawkins in the loss of a loving daughter." (The Weekly Arizona Miner; Prescott; January 31,1879; page 3.)

DAVID ERASTUS HAWKINS: (b. 11-08-1851, Independence, MO) died in Prescott March 26, 1882 and is buried in the Hawkins plot. Talitha Cumi (Bristow) Hawkins married "Doc" Wilbur.

WILLIAM HENRY HAWKINS (b. 02-28-1820, Tennessee) husband of Harriet, was a Confederate soldier in Wood's Regiment, Missouri Cavalry, Company D. He died January 26, 1883, and is buried with his family.

LOUISA JANE HAWKINS (b. 02-10-1865, Independence, MO) married James Alvin Van Deren at Cherry on July 4, 1880. They were parents of 3 daughters when she died in 1887. He married Edith Mae Strahan, and they became parents of 2 daughters and 1 son.

JAMES GABRIEL HAWKINS: Married Mariah May

Dickinson on July 3, 1882. They were the parents of 2 children when she died in Camp Verde in 1889. Constable James Hawkins was shot and killed by a prisoner in his custody in Jerome on April 19, 1891. Her parents, Samuel Cotton and Nancy Jane (Green) Dickinson, who had been part of the "1875 Wagon Train," raised the orphans; Charles became a cowboy and married Francis Bruce, and Minnie married Maurice Calvin Smith. The Dickinson family with Maurice and Minnie Smith, owned and operated the Cottonwood store and post office until they sold out to Alonzo Mason, who became postmaster May 21, 1907.

LURA BELLE HAWKINS: (b. 1863, Belton, MO) married Dennis Hickey. She died of complications during childbirth in April of 1892 and is buried next to "our babies" and her husband, a miner, who died in Jerome on July 28, 1909.

HARRIET (HATTIE) MELISSA STRATON HAWKINS (b. 10-07-1827, Tennessee) died in Jerome December 20, 1895, and is buried next to her husband, William, and her children. Harriet M. Hawkins was granted a land patent for 155.6 acres near what became Tuzigoot, on September 3, 1884. When she died, only 4 sons were living; Emory, William, Lee and Tom and two sons-in-law, Dennis Hickey and James Van Deren. (AUTHOR'S NOTE: According to the Hawkins Family Genealogy prepared by Alice Hawkins Gamble from the Mormon Temple Archives Harriet's maiden name was STAYTON.)

THOMAS ALEXANDER HAWKINS: (b. 06-02-1871, Belton MO) DROWNED IN Mockingbird Wash, Hayfield Draw, July 25, 1901. (see: The Verde Independent; "1901: DROWNED IN CLOUDBURST; Thomas Hawkins;" July 24, 2012.)

EMERY (EMORY) WASHINGTON HAWKINS: (b. 03-15-1869, Independence, MO) married Frances Moser in

Flagstaff on June 28, 1897. He died in 1905.

WILLIAM HENRY HAWKINS, JR.: (b. 02-07-1855) was granted a land patent for 120 acres near the family homestead of his mother, on February 8, 1900. He died in Watts, Los Angeles, California on June 27, 1927 (may not be in the Cottonwood cemetery).

LEE ANDREW JACKSON HAWKINS (B. 01-02-1867, Independence, MO) was a dentist in Jerome. He married Ethel Jane Carrier. His photographs are lasting reminders of what Jerome and neighboring areas once were. He died January 6, 1932.

See: The Verde Independent; "1875: VERDE RESERVATION OPEN TO SETTLEMENT; Wagon Trains Arrive;" August 22, 2012

APPENDIX #4
Hawkins Family Land Transactions

Source: Yavapai County Courthouse, Prescott, Arizona
E. W. Hawkins to H. M. Hawkins
Book 39 p. 47
160 acres of land

T. A. Hawkins to E. W. Hawkins
Book 39 p. 379
80 acres of land

E. W. Hawkins to Thomas A. Hawkins
Book 39 p. 394
80 acres of land, April 1896

E. W. and T. A. Hawkins to R. A. Windes
Book 34 p. 141
80 acres of land, April 1896

E. W. to T. A. Hawkins
Book 41, p. 274
Mine exchange

AUTHOR'S NOTE: I looked up one of these transactions in the County Recorder's office to see if this land was near Tuzigoot National Monument. It was right where my Grandma Jennie said it was. The description of the property was as follows:

South 1/2 of the NW 1/4 of Section 22 in Township 16, north of range 3, each of Gila and Salt River meridian in Arizona - 80 acres.

Additional Note: The Gila and Salt River Meridian, the central point in Arizona where all land measurements originate, is located near where Robert and Jennie Holmes homesteaded from 1907 to 1923.

APPENDIX #5
Newspaper article from Jerome Reporter, August 1, 1901.
(Submitted by Camp Verde Historical Society)

THOMAS A. HAWKINS
Loses his Life Attempting to Cross an Arroya(sic) Filled with Water. Drowned by a cloudburst. Untimely End of a Popular and Well Known Young Cattleman

Thursday afternoon, July 25, the news reached Jerome that Thomas A. Hawkins had been drowned, and the particulars of the unusually sad affair are about as follows:

Hawkins and Ed Walker had located some mining claims in the Cherry Creek country that afternoon, and were returning to Aultman when the accident occurred. They had reached the Mocking Bird wash, in the Cherry Creek road, about fourteen miles from Jerome, and three miles from Aultman, and found the wash running full of water. Hawkins wanted to drive the horse and buggy through the raging current, but was persuaded not to do so by Walker. Hawkins unhitched the horse from the buggy and rode out into the stream for the purpose of testing its depth, and had gone about 50 feet from the bank when the horse fell with him. Hawkins fell on the upper side of the horse and, it is supposed, that the raging current washed him under the horse.

The next that Walker saw of him he was below the horse, about the middle of the stream, and was striking the water with both hands, as if trying to keep his head above the water. Walker ran along the bank and called to him, encouraging him to keep his head above the water, but Hawkins appeared to be dazed, and did not answer or turn his head. He sank fifty feet below where the horse fell with him.

Hawkins' body was found about a quarter of a mile below the scene of the accident. Upon examination of the body it was found that he had received a severe contusion on the left temple when he fell from the horse.

Walker hurried to Aultman and secured assistance, and the remains were taken to his house at that place and prepared for burial.

Hawkins was 30 years of age, having been born on June 15, 1871, and had lived in the Verde Valley near all his life.

Hawkins was engaged to marry Miss Rhoda Marr of Aultman, and the wedding was to have taken place about August 10. He had his home nearly completed for his bride when death ended his plans.

It is not known exactly what his estate is worth, but it is estimated to be in the neighborhood of $10,000, and as yet is is not known whether he left a will or not.

Three brothers survive him--Dr. L. A. Hawkins, the dentist of Jerome; Emery Hawkins of Cottonwood, and William Hawkins of Clear Creek, all good, substantial citizens of Yavapai County.

The remains were interred at Cottonwood Friday, in his wedding suit, by the side of father, mother, three brothers and three sisters.

The following brief history of the death of members of this once large and well known family will be of interest to readers of the Reporter:

--John Hawkins, age 18, was killed in 1876 by being thrown from a horse.

--Erastus Hawkins, another brother, died suddenly from some unknown cause in 1880.

--W. H. Hawkins, the father, died in 1885, caused by drinking poison by mistake.

--Mrs. James Alderson, a sister, was burned to death in 1878.

--Mrs. J. A. Van Deren, a sister, died with fever in 1887.

--Mrs. Dennis Hickey, a sister, died in child-birth in 1888.

--James Hawkins, a brother, was killed in 1891 by Tom Gallagher, in Jerome, while acting as peace officer. Gallagher was sent to prison for life, but was pardoned and died in Tucson a short time afterwards.

--Mrs. W. H. Hawkins, mother, died in 1895.

APPENDIX #6
Family Record #1

APPENDIX #7
Family Record #2

Family record of Jennie's parents and brothers and sisters in her own handwriting. Submitted by William Henry Holmes, Jennie's son.

APPENDIX #8
Family Record #3

Family record of Jennie, her husband and children. When she refers to "St. Johns, Arizona," she means that the children were born on the homestead near Cashion.

> Family Record.
> Parents
> John Robert Holmes born Jan 30. 1881. England
> Jennie Lee Holmes born Feb. 26. 1891. Arizona
> Children
> George Holmes born Nov 26. 1907 died Nov 26. St. John 1907
> Henry Holmes born Sept 26. 1908 died Sept 26. St. John 19
> Mabel Bell Holmes born Sept 10. 1910. Pho
> Mary Alice Holmes born July 11. 1912. Pho
> Robert Ullock Holmes born Aug. 13. 1914 St. johns
> James Wilson Holmes born June 12. 1917 Pho
> Step Myrtle Edna Holmes born Feb. 1. 1900. St Johns
> William Henry Holmes born Dec. 16. 1921. St John
>
> Mother was married when sixteen years old
> ived at Arlington A ina first year
> She moved to St. John. Arizona

APPENDIX #9
Biographical sketch of Dr. Lee Hawkins

Arizona – Prehistoric-Aboriginal-Pioneer-Modern
Biographical
Volume III (Published in 1916)

L.A. HAWKINS, D.D.S.

The enviable reputation which Dr. L. A. Hawkins enjoys today throughout Arizona as an able, reliable and successful dentist has been earned through thirty years of continuous practice of his profession in this state, the first seven of which were spent in traveling from place to place and the last twenty-three at Jerome, where he still makes his home. He is truly one of the pioneers of the community, for his settlement here antedated the foundation of the city and his high standing in the eyes of the people at large is sufficient evidence that his life has been at all times honorable, upright and straightforward.

The Doctor was born in Missouri in 1867 and is son of W. H. and H. M. Hawkins, who came overland to Arizona in 1875, locating in Verde Valley, where the father turned his attention to the cattle business. Pioneer conditions prevailed everywhere, the Indians being hostile and numerous, but in spite of these obstacles and difficulties W. H. Hawkins was successful in the conduct of his ranch, both parents remaining thereon until their deaths.

Dr. Hawkins acquired his early education in the Arizona public schools and after studying dentistry took a post graduate course in Chicago, entering immediately afterward upon the practice of his profession in this state. He has the distinction of being the oldest continuous practitioner in Arizona and each year of the thirty during which he has been active has brought him increased patronage and added distinction in his chosen field. For a time, he worked in various parts of Arizona, traveling from place to place with his instruments, and he also maintained offices in different cities, including Phoenix and Globe. Eventually, however, he located on the present site of Jerome, coming here before the city was founded, and for the past twenty-three years he has remained one of the representative and honored citizens of the community. His practice increased rapidly as his skill and ability became widely known, and outside the line of his profession he is interested in everything that pertains to the welfare and growth of the city and to its material, intellectual or moral upbuilding. For many years he has had charge of the weather bureau at Jerome and his work in this capacity has been done with his usual efficiency and ability.

In 1890 Dr. Hawkins married Miss E. J. Carrier, a daughter of Dr. M. A. Carrier, a native of New York and a pioneer in Arizona. They have become the parents of one son. The Doctor is affiliated with the Masonic Lodge and the Order of the Eastern Star and gives his political allegiance to the Democratic party. He was one of the true pioneers in Jerome, having witnessed the entire development of the city, and he is widely and favorably known, his genuine personal worth and sterling qualities of character having gained for him the respect and confidence of all who are associated with him. In November, 1915, he was elected president of the Arizona Dental Society, which fact indicates his high standing in the profession.

APPENDIX #10
Robert and Jennie Holmes marriage license

Marriage License.

To any Regularly Licensed or Ordained Minister of the Gospel, any Judge of a Court of Record, or any Justice of the Peace within this County:

You are hereby authorized to solemnize the Rites of Matrimony between _John Robert Holmes_ of _Maricopa_ County _Arizona_ and _Jennie Lee Hawkins_ of _Maricopa_ County, _Arizona_, and endorse the same on this License and make return thereof to this office according to law.

IN WITNESS WHEREOF, I have hereunto set my hand and affixed my official seal this _17th_ day of _November_ A. D. 190_6_.

George Kirkland
Clerk of the Probate Court of _Maricopa_ County, Arizona Territory.

Marriage Certificate.

THIS CERTIFIES, that on the _18th_ day of _Nov_ A. D. 190_6_ _John Robert Holmes_ and _Jennie Lee Hawkins_ were united in marriage at _Phoenix_ according to the laws of Arizona Territory and by the authority of the foregoing License, by _J.C. Phillips_ in the presence of _George Henry_ and _Mrs. C.W. McAnally_ who have hereto attached their signatures as witnesses to said marriage ceremony.

IN WITNESS WHEREOF, the said contracting parties, the said witnesses and the said _J.C. Phillips_, who solemnized such marriage ceremony, have hereunto set their hands, this _18th_ day of _Nov._ A. D. 190_6_.

George Henry, Witness.
Mrs. C.W. McAnally, Witness.
John Robert Holmes, Contracting Party.
Jennie Lee Hawkins, Contracting Party.
J.C. Phillips, Officer, Minister or Person Performing Ceremony.

NOTE—Persons filling out above Certificate must be careful and get full names of all parties, and see that they sign their full names.

No. 301.—MARRIAGE LICENSE.—The H. H. McNeil Company's Red-Line Blanks, Phoenix, Arizona.

APPENDIX #11
Letter from Rev. & Mrs. Charles Olvey from Orinoco River Mission

Home Office:
Box 611, South Pasadena
California 91030

THE ORINOCO RIVER MISSION
VENEZUELA, SOUTH AMERICA

January, 1968

Dear Friends,

A celebration--October 24th! On that date in 1937 we sailed out of Los Angeles harbor for Venezuela. Same date in 1967 we flew into New York in just 4½ hours from Maiquetía. Thirty years spent along the Orinoco River--and every year a blessing in His service.

Furlough time means fellowship time: Friends, families, services in the churches that support us by prayer and giving, the making of many new friendships, becoming acquainted with new and complex freeways, new gadgets, stateside foods, visits to dentists, new glasses, seeing doctors--and ever so many new experiences.

Many of you have asked about our girls. Lynn and husband Pierino (Salerno) are in Venezuela and contemplate a trip to the States this year. Salma and Al (Gusiff) are living in Whittier, California where we can enjoy their three children from time to time.

1967 was a year we will long remember. Here are a few "high-lights": A letter from the witchdoctor (a living miracle) who found the Lord in the Maquiritare village, sharing Christian greetings of his tribe. The visit of Pastor Arnold Hickock who brought real blessing to us and to the many Christians who knew him. A wonderful trip of ministry on the mission launch "Buena Esperanza" into virgin territory to wind up our four years on the field. And then, on October 6, the sudden Home-going of Pilot Don Roberson of M.A.F. and Curt Findley when the plane went down in back jungle country, and our participation in the search. Then the funeral. We can only bow to God's will.

We would like to tell you more--and show you too. From now until the time of our return to Venezuela in September we will be available to represent our work with The Orinoco River Mission in Venezuela. There are colored slides of the Indian and River work, 16mm movies and cultural items. In late Spring we plan a deputation trip into the Pacific Northwest. Let us hear from you.

We take this opportunity to express our sincere thanks for your many cards and letters received during the holiday season.

Sincerely in Him,

Charles and Mary

Rev. & Mrs. Charles W. Olvey
344 North 20th Drive
Phoenix, Arizona 85009

APPENDIX #12
Letter of condolence to Jennie from Congressman John J. Rhodes

JOHN J. RHODES
1ST DISTRICT, ARIZONA

COMMITT[EE]
APPROPRIA[TIONS]

Congress of the United States
House of Representatives
Washington, D. C.

November 19, 1962

Mrs. John R. Holmes
1746 West Buchanan
Phoenix, Arizona

Dear Mrs. Holmes:

    Please accept my condolences on the loss that has come to you through the death of your husband.

    I realize there is little anyone can say to offer comfort at such a time of sorrow but I want you to know that you and your family have my deepest sympathy in your bereavement.

Yours sincerely,

John J. Rhodes

APPENDIX #13
Newspaper Clipping from Cottonwood Independent, February 1981

APS DISMANTLES 60-YEAR-OLD BRIDGE OVER VERDE RIVER AT TAPCO PLANT

By Bill Graffius, Cottonwood Independent Staff Writer

The swinging bridge crossing the Verde River near the old TAPCO (The Arizona Power Company) plant northwest of Clarkdale on the Sycamore Canyon Road was torn down by Arizona Public Service Co. workmen last week. According to Cottonwood APS representative Frank Wolfe, the local landmark, which has crossed the sometimes turbulent Verde since the 1920s, was removed by APS because of "a lot of concern on the liability of the thing." Wolfe also cited vandalism at the aging TAPCO facility and the removal of the caretaker at the plant as reasons for dismantling the bridge.

APS public relations representative, Pete Klute said, in a telephone interview Tuesday, that the decision to remove the bridge came about "fairly recently" during a regular review of company properties for the purpose of foreseeing liability problems. "As far as the liability side," Klute said, "I know the company has been looking at all its property, particularly substations." Complicating the liability question, Klute said, was the fact that the bridge is located on private property owned by Phelps Dodge Corporation.

The TAPCO plant, constructed in 1917, formerly provided 8.5 megawatts of electricity to residences, businesses, mines and smelting operations in the Verde Valley. The plant went off-line in 1951, but was refurbished and brought back on-line for four days in 1959 when a power outage interrupted electric service to the Valley. Since then the TAPCO facility has served as a switching substation providing power to the area along Sycamore Canyon Road.

The swinging bridge was originally constructed to provide access for TAPCO employees to the plant during times of high water on the Verde. Following the plant's shut-down, the bridge was maintained to provide high-water access for the caretaker housed adjacent to the facility. The caretaker position was eliminated in 1980, and Klute said that because there is no longer a caretaker at the plant, the bridge was no longer necessary.

Klute, like Wolfe, also cited vandalism problems at the plant as a reason for removing the bridge, and added that costs for keeping the bridge in repair were no longer justifiable because the plant was no longer in use and the caretaker had been removed.

TAPCO Power Plant on the Verde River as it looks in 2018.

APPENDIX #14
Obituary for Mrs. Harriet M. Hawkins

From Obituary Book at Sharlot Hall Museum, Prescott, Arizona, December 1895

In Memoriam

Last Friday night, 20th inst., Mrs. Harriet M. Hawkins of the Upper Verde, departed this life at the age of 68, after a very long and painful illness. During the last six months Mrs. Hawkins has been confined to her bed with a paralytic affection that has afflicted her more or less for the past two years, a great deal of the time having a wandering mind and moving around the room with much difficulty by the help of a cane. Last June she became confined to her bed and since that time she has had to be cared for constantly by nurses and her faithful sons and sons-in-law. Her beloved Emory, who has so long been at home with his mother, steadily looked after all her wants--often times seen by the writer in the saddle riding the country on the hunt for another nurse to succeed the last one. Day after day, week after week, and month after month, barely having time to do the chores. Her beloved William coming from his ranch, two or three miles away, every night for weeks at a time to perform his duties of love to a suffering mother. Never will he forget the farewell embraces he has stooped over to receive before returning to his home. Her beloved Lee making his weekly visits from his dental rooms at Jerome, seven miles away. "Mother can't bear for me to miss once," I've heard him say. Her beloved Tom coming from the cattle ranges often to do all in his power under the circumstances--to be of comfort to the one who loved as her baby.

Her sons-in-law, Messrs. Hickey and James Van Deren, deserve much credit for the many nights and days they have spent lifting around that suffering body like that of a child and doing thousands of things for her help and comfort.

Much gratitude is felt by the family to the faithful nurses who have toiled through these months with much patience. In a very special manner is Mrs. Keene, the last nurse, who watched with the mother to the last, remembered with pleasure and gratitude.

It is generally the case that when chronic sickness is in the neighborhood and becomes a fixture that the neighbors lapse into more or less neglect; but the family takes pleasure in remembering especially Mrs. Ricker, who was cut short in her kindness by her own sickness and death. Also, Mrs. Will Van Deren, who was faithful to the end. Such is a noble quality.

Mrs. Hawkins' afflictions were exceptionally severe before her bodily ailments. Nearly twenty years ago she, with her husband and most of her children, emigrated from Missouri to this valley. During that time she has mourned the loss of her husband, five daughters and four sons. Ten deaths, and four of them by sad accidents. Only four sons of that large family are left to mourn all these losses.

At last her painful sufferings are over and the weary soul is at rest. She has had enough of trouble; now may the giver of all good things give her enough of rest. For about forty years she was a steadfast Christian and member of the Baptist Church.

William Henry and Harriet Hawkins are buried in the Cottonwood Cemetery along with many of the Hawkins family members.

APPENDIX #15
Newspaper Article on the day Myrtle died and William Henry (Billie) was born.

BIRTH, DEATH AND ACCIDENT COME TO FAMILY SAME DAY

Shortly after the wife of Deputy Sheriff Robert Holmes, special guard for county prisoners working in the chain gang, had presented him with a fine 8-pound boy at their home south of Cashion, Mr. Holmes received word of the death of his eldest daughter, Mrs. Lawrence Conley, at St. Joseph's hospital following an operation. About an hour later James Wilson Holmes, four-year-old son of Mr. Holmes, sustained an injury to his left eye which may cause the loss of the sight of the eye.

According to Mr. Holmes, the little lad was attempting to chop a piece of wood with a hatchet when a splinter flew up and struck him in the left eye. The blow bursted a blood vessel and possibly injured the nerves of the eye. Dr. William A. Schwartz, who attended the injury, stated he had hopes of saving the sight.

The new arrival in the Holmes family has been named William Henry and both mother and the babe are reported doing nicely.

Mrs. Conley was born in Phoenix and was 21 years old. She was the only daughter of Mr. Holmes by a former wife. Mrs. Conley was a graduate of the Tempe Normal school and is well known in Phoenix and the valley. She became the wife of Lawrence Conley of Liberty more than two years ago and leaves beside her husband, a boy, Lawrence Conley, Jr., one year old. Mrs. Conley also is survived by her father and stepmother and two brothers, Robert Holmes, Jr., and James Wilson Holmes, and two sisters, Mabel Holmes and Mary Holmes.

Funeral services will be held at 10 o'clock this morning in the church at Liberty and burial will be in the Liberty cemetery.

BIBLIOGRAPHY

Public Collections
Sharlot Hall Archives, Prescott
Phoenix Public Library
Central Arizona Historical Society, Phoenix
Arizona State University Library: Arizona Collection, Tempe
Tempe Historical Society
Camp Verde Historical Society
Jerome State Historic Park
Jerome Historical Society
Arizona Capital Archives, Phoenix
Fort Verde State Park, Camp Verde
Dead Horse Ranch State Park, Cottonwood
Sedona Library
Sedona Historical Society
Yavapai County Courthouse, Prescott
Cottonwood Cemetery
Tuzigoot National Monument, Clarkdale

Private Collections
Mabel Holmes Stierwalt
Mary Holmes Olvey
William Henry Holmes
Madeline Stierwalt Wallace
Zoe Ann Holmes Ravert
Zona Lee Holmes Finney
Wyona Holmes Jaffe
Mary Belle Stierwalt Garner
Violet Hopkins Holmes

Interviews
Jennie Hawkins Holmes
Mabel Holmes Stierwalt, daughter of Jennie
Mary Holmes Olvey - daughter of Jennie
William Henry Holmes, son of Jennie
Bernice Brogdon Holmes, wife of William Holmes
Violet Hopkins Holmes, mother of Wyona Jaffe
Harriett Fern Hawkins, daughter of Emery Hawkins, Jennie's uncle
Lorena Udall Hawkins, wife of grandson of Emery Hawkins
Richard Pickering, half-brother to Fern Hawkins
Nancy Smith, curator of Jerome Historical Society
Margaret Hallett, Camp Verde Historical Society
Mary Belle Stierwalt Garner, Madeline Stierwalt Wallace, and Margaret Stierwalt Beatty, daughters of Mabel Stierwalt
Herbert V. Young, Arizona historian and author of They Came to Jerome and Water by the Inch
Earl Van Deren, nephew of James Van Deren who was married to Louisa Hawkins, Jennie's aunt
Agnes Ramsey, granddaughter of James Gabriel Hawkins, Jennie's uncle

BOOKS

Arizona Adventure; Action-Packed True Tales of Early Arizona: Marshall Trimble; Golden West Publishers; Phoenix, AZ, 1982.

Arizona Handbook: Bill Weir, Moon Publications, 1986.

Arizona Highways Album - The Road to Statehood: Dean Smith, Ed.; Arizona Department of Transportation; State of Arizona; 1987.

Arizona: Its People and Resources: Members of the Faculty of University of Arizona, University of Arizona Press, Tucson, AZ; 1972.

Arizona Territorial Cookbook: The Food and Lifestyles of a Frontier: Melissa Ruffner Weiner and Budge Ruffner, Donning Co. Pub.; Norfolk/Virginia Beach; 1982.

Arizona, the Youngest State: Biographical Volume III: S. J. Clark Pub. Co.; Chicago, 1916.

Cottonwood, Clarkdale, and Cornville History: Cottonwood Chapter 2021; American Association of Retired Persons; Revised Edition; 1985.

Dust in Our Desks:; Territory Days to the Present in Arizona Schools: Allen Pace Nilsen with Margaret Ferry and L. J. Evans; Arizona State University Collection of Education; Tempe, AZ, 1985.

Filaree: A Novel of an American Life: Marguerite Noble; University of New Mexico Press; 1979.

The Lunch Tree: Irene Cornwall Cofer; Mohave Pioneers Historical Society, Inc.; Theo. Gaus Sons, Inc.; Brooklyn, NY; 1969.

A Passion For Freedom: The Life of Sharlot Hall: Margaret F. Mitchell; The University of Arizona Press; Tucson, AZ; 1982.

Phoenix 1870 - 1970: Herb and Dorothy McLaughlin; Arizona Photographic Association, Inc.; Phoenix, AZ; 1970.

Pioneer Stories of Arizona's Verde Valley: Verde Valley Pioneers Association; 1954.

They Came to Jerome: The Billion Dollar Copper Camp: Herbert V. Young; Jerome Historical Society; 1972.

Those Early Days: The Sedona Westerners; The Verde Independent; 1975.

Water by the Inch: Herbert V. Young; Northland Press, Flagstaff, AZ; 1982.

Pamphlets

Informational pamphlet from Ft. Verde State Park, Courtesy of State Park Service

INDEX

Adams, Mrs. Robert J. (Roberta Lea Holmes)	69, 78, 81, 83, 84
Agua Fria River	27
Ajo (AZ)	72
Alderson, Mrs. James (Sarah Hawkins)	18
Antelope Hill (AZ)	20
Arizona Light & Power Co.	54
Arizona Republican	64
Arizona State Hospital (Flagstaff)	24
Arizona State Hospital (Phoenix)	25
Arizona Territory	7, 8, 11, 13, 16, 20, 26, 37
Arlington (AZ)	27, 28, 33, 34, 37
Ashfork (AZ)	64
Aultman (AZ)	14
Bancroft, Roy	66
Baptist, (Miss)	55
Bartlett Dam (Verde River)	34, 67, 68
Beatty, Mrs. Thomas (Margaret Faye Stierwalt)	63, 64, 78, 79
Beaver Creek (AZ)	10
Bell, Dr.	26
Belvedere (CA)	51
Big Dry Wash (AZ)	22
Bisbee (AZ)	57
Bloody Basin (AZ)	83
Brashear, Jay	37
Brewer, Blanche	29
Brewer, Hugh 29 Brewer, Mrs. Hugh (Ella Louise Hawkins)	19, 20, 29
Brewer, Walter	29
Brightwell, Mr.	55
Bristow, Pleasant	11

Bristow, J. O.	11
Brogdon, Bernice "Bernie" (Mrs. Wm H. Holmes)	72, 73, 87, 88
Buckeye (AZ)	8, 29, 30, 36, 37, 48, 52, 54, 73
Bunger, Mr.	52
Camp Callan (CA)	72
Camp Lincoln (AZ)	21
Camp Verde (AZ)	12, 21, 22, 23
Capitol Church (Phoenix)	67
Carrier, Ethyl (Mrs. Lee A. Hawkins)	17, 18
Carrier, Myron Dr.	17
Casa Grande (AZ)	67
Cashion (AZ)	8, 38, 42, 45, 46, 47
Cherry Creek (AZ)	14, 20
Civilian Conservation Corps (CCC)	67
Clarkdale (AZ)	20
Clear Creek (AZ)	10, 21, 24
Cleveland, Helen	57
Cold Water (AZ)	27
Conley, Lawrence	42
Conley, Mrs. Lawrence (Myrtle Edna Holmes)	34, 39, 40, 42, 44
Conley, Robert Lawrence "Larry"	42
Cook, Reverend	67
Cottonwood (AZ)	11, 20, 21, 23, 29
Crook, George (General)	21
Crook Trail (AZ)	11
Davis, Mrs.	40
Dead Horse Ranch State Park (Cottonwood AZ)	11, 12
DeBerge & Babcock Electric/DeBerge & Holmes Electric	27, 68, 71, 72, 73
Dickenson (Family)	11
Dickenson, Mrs. Charles	15

Ellis Island (NY)	36
England, Dalton-in-Furness	34, 35, 36
Finney Mrs. Robert (Zona Lee Holmes)	73, 88
Flagstaff, (AZ)	24, 25, 57, 58, 59
Fort Apache (AZ)	21, 22
Fort Verde Historic Museum	12
Fort Whipple (Prescott)	21
Gallagher, Tom	14
Garner, Mrs. John (Mary Belle Stierwalt)	34, 63, 64, 78, 79
Garrido, Mrs. Miguel (Melinda Suzanne "Susie" Holmes)	69
Gibbons, Merle (Mrs. James Wilson Holmes)	34, 61, 70
Gila Bend (AZ)	72
Gila River (AZ)	38, 44
Globe (AZ)	21, 57
Goff, Mrs.	55
Grumbles, Mrs.	55
Gusiff, Albert	66
Gusiff, Mrs. Albert (Salma Souki)	66
Hawaii	17
Hawkins, Albert Bruce	20
Hawkins, Alvin Zebedee	8, 19, 25, 26, 29, 38
Hawkins, Bell L.	18
Hawkins, David Erastus	14
Hawkins, Dollie	18
Hawkins, Ella Louise (Mrs. Hugh Brewer)	19, 20, 29
Hawkins, Emery Washington	14, 16, 24, 26
Hawkins, Harriet Jane "Hattie" (Mrs. Jay H. Russell)	8, 19, 25, 26, 29
Hawkins, James Gabriel	14
Hawkins, Jennie Lee (Mrs. John Robert Holmes) Referred to throughout the book	1-117
Hawkins, John Sylvester	14

Hawkins, Lee Andrew (Dr.)	13, 16, 17, 18, 20
Hawkins, Louisa J. (Mrs. James Van Deren)	19
Hawkins, Lura Belle (Mrs. Dennis Hickey)	19
Hawkins, Mary Alice (Mrs. Edd McAnally)	8, 19, 25, 31, 33, 34, 64
Hawkins, Myron	17
Hawkins, Ollie Viola (Mrs. William Henry Hawkins, Jr.)	51
Hawkins, Ophie (Mrs. William Aaron Hawkins)	66
Hawkins, Pendleton Guy	19, 20
Hawkins, Sarah (Mrs. James Alderson)	19
Hawkins, Thomas Alexander	14, 16, 26
Hawkins, Verde Vernell "Verd"	19, 20, 29, 87
Hawkins, Verna (Mrs. Robert Campbell)	40
Hawkins, Virginia Belle (Mrs. John Morris)	19, 20
Hawkins, William Aaron "Bill"	8, 19, 25, 26, 29 30, 31, 51, 66
Hawkins, William Henry, Sr.	8, 11, 26
Hawkins, William Henry, Jr.	8, 18, 19, 25, 28, 51
Hawkins, Mrs. Wm. Henry Jr. (Alice Smith)	8, 14, 19, 20
Hayden Mill (Tempe)	28
Haynes Mine	30
Henry, Alice (Mrs. John Robert Holmes)	34, 54
Henry, George	53
Henry, Lucinda "Sinda" or "Cindy" (Mrs. George Henry)	53, 54, 57, 60
Henry, Willard	54
Hickey, Mrs. Dennis (Lura Belle Hawkins)	19
Hideaway Court (Prescott)	68
Hohokam Indians	51
Holmes, Ada (Mrs. Edward Wetzler)	33, 36
Holmes, Agnes (Mrs. John G. Montgomery)	36, 45

Holmes, Arthur Edward "Eddie"	69
Holmes, Gary Joseph	69
Holmes, George	38, 39
Holmes, Henry	38, 39
Holmes, James	35, 36, 37, 44, 45
Holmes, Mrs. James (Mary Ullock)	35, 36, 37
Holmes, James Wilson "Pinkie"	1-117
Holmes, Mrs. James Wilson (Margaret "Peggy" Walsh)	71
Holmes, Mrs. James Wilson, (Merle Gibbons)	34, 61, 70, 71
Holmes, James Wellington "Jimmie"	34, 66, 70, 71
Holmes, John Charles	69
Holmes John Robert	1-117
Holmes, Mrs. John Robert (Alice Henry)	34, 54
Holmes, Mrs. John Robert (Jennie Lee Hawkins)	1-117
Holmes, Kevin Bruce	69
Holmes, Mabel Belle (Mrs. Roy Stierwalt)	1-117
Holmes, Mary Alice (Mrs. Charles Olvey)	1-117
Holmes, Mary Christene (Mrs. Tom McKnight)	69, 81, 83, 85
Holmes, Melinda Suzanne (Mrs. Miguel Garrido)	69
Holmes, Myrtle Edna "Bea" (Mrs. Lawrence Conley)	34, 39, 40, 42, 44
Holmes, Nancy Gayle	69
Holmes, Robert Ullock, Sr. "Bobbie"	1-117
Holmes, Mrs. Robert Ullock, Jr. (Violet Christine Hopkins)	34, 67, 68, 70, 82
Holmes, Robert Ullock, Jr.	69
Holmes, Roberta Lea (Mrs. Robert J. Adams)	69, 83
Holmes, Sarah	36
Holmes, William Henry "Bill"	1-117
Holmes, Mrs. William Henry (Bernice "Bernie" Brogdon)	72, 73, 87, 88
Holmes, Wyona Mae (Mrs. Irv Jaffe)	1-117

Holmes, Zena Rae (Mrs. Ronald Smith)	73, 89
Holmes, Zoe Ann (Mrs. Jerry Ravert)	73, 86
Holmes, Zona Lee (Mrs. Robert Finney)	73, 88
Holton, Miss	55
Hopkins, Violet Christine (Mrs. Robert Ullock Holmes, Sr.)	34, 67, 68, 70, 72
Humans, James	11
Hutchinson (Family)	11
Jaffe, Irving	69
Jaffe, Mrs. Irving (Wyona Mae Holmes)	1-117
Jerome (AZ)	14, 16, 17, 18, 20, 29
Johnson, R. V. (Reverend)	64, 65
Johnson, Riley	29
Jordan, W. A.	15
Lake Montezuma (AZ)	7
Luke Air Force Base (AZ)	73
Manila (Philippines)	72
Marana (AZ)	64, 72
Maricopa Creamery (Tempe)	28
Marr, Rhoda	14
Marshall Lake (Flagstaff)	58, 59, 60
Mauzy, Miss	55
Maxwell, Minnie	24
Mayer (AZ)	20
McAnally, Edd	25
McAnally, Mrs. Edd (Mary Alice Hawkins)	8, 19, 25, 31, 33, 34, 64
McBride, Judy	6
McKnight, Mrs. Thomas (Mary Christene Holmes)	69, 81, 83, 85
Midzor, John	52
Midzor, Steve	52
Miller, Walter	17

Mitchell, (Mr. & Mrs.)	45
Mockingbird Creek (AZ)	14
Mogollon Rim (AZ)	21, 68
Montgomery, John G	45
Montgomery, Mrs. John G. (Agnes Holmes)	36, 45
Montgomery Stadium (Phoenix)	56
Moore, Bill	27
Mormon Lake (Flagstaff)	57
Mormon Mountain (Flagstaff)	59
New State Electric (Phoenix)	72
Oak Creek (Sedona)	10, 24
Olvey, Charles Wesley "Chuck" (Reverend)	34, 52, 56, 64, 65, 66, 82
Olvey, Mrs. Charles (Mary Alice Holmes)	1-117
Olvey, May (Charles Olvey's mother)	57
Orinoco River Mission (Venezuela, S.A.)	65
Orpheum Theatre (Phoenix)	48, 56
Parker (AZ)	88
Parkman, I. H.	37
Peck's Lake (Verde Valley)	16, 19
Phoenix (AZ)	1-117
Pilgrim's Playground (Mormon Lake)	57, 58
Pine Lawn Court (Prescott)	57, 60
Prescott (AZ)	12, 13, 20, 21, 57, 60, 68
Prussell, Evelyn "Lynn" (Mrs. Pierno Salerno)	66
Purtyman, Clara	24
Ramsey, Agnes	17
Ravert, Jerry	86
Ravert, Mrs. Jerry (Zoe Ann Holmes)	73, 86
Red Rock (AZ)	24
Reeder, Deborah Lynn	4, 7, 5, 90
Rialto Theatre (Phoenix)	56

Ritter, Mrs.	554
Roberts, Mrs. (Turney)	46, 54, 55
Roosevelt Dam (AZ)	26
Russell, Mrs. Jay (Harriet Jane "Hattie" Hawkins)	8, 19, 25, 26, 29
Russell, Lillian	39, 40
S. S. California	66
St. Johns (near Cashion, AZ)	34
St. Johns Indian Mission	38
Salerno, Pierno	66
Salerno, Mrs. Pierno (Evelyn "Lynn" Prussell)	66
Salt River (AZ)	20, 26, 28, 38, 44, 68
Salt River Valley (AZ)	26
San Carlos Indian Reservation (AZ)	12, 21, 22
Schools	
Adams School (renamed Grace Court School) Phoenix	55
Arizona Sate College (Arizona State University) Tempe	64
Biola Institute (CA) (Biola University)	65
Cashion School (Cashion)	64
Five Points School (Phoenix)	25
Jackson School (Phoenix)	54, 55
Middle Verde School (Verde Valley)	24
Murphy School (Phoenix)	84
North Phoenix High School	72
Phoenix Union High School	50, 55, 67, 72
St. Johns School District (Cashion)	54
Tempe Normal School	42, 45
University of Oklahoma (Norman, OK)	65
West Phoenix High School	56
Schuerman, Henry	24
Sieber, Al	22

Smith, Alice (Mrs. William H. Hawkins, Jr.)	8, 14, 19, 20
Smith, Mrs. Ronald (Zena Rae Holmes)	89
Smith, Tom	11
Souki, Salma (Mrs. Albert Gusiff)	66
South Mountain Park (Phoenix)	83
Stayton, Harriet M. (Mrs. William H. Hawkins, Sr.)	8, 11, 26
Stierwalt, Madeline Lee (Mrs. George Wallace)	34, 63, 64, 77, 78
Stierwalt, Margaret Faye (Mrs. Thomas Beatty)	63, 64, 78, 79, 83
Stierwalt, Mary Belle (Mrs. John Garner)	34, 63, 64, 78, 79, 83
Stierwalt, Roy	34, 63, 64, 70, 81
Stierwalt, Mrs. Roy (Mabel Belle Holmes)	1-117
Stoneman Lake (AZ)	58
Sugarloaf Mountain (AZ)	83
Sunset Crater (AZ	58
Sycamore Creek (AZ)	83
TAPCO Power Plant (Verde Valley)	19, 20
Tempe (AZ)	28
Thayer, Doctor	30, 42
Tombstone (AZ)	57
Trusdale, Miss	55
Tucson (AZ)	12, 13, 14, 57
Tuzigoot National Monument (Cottonwood)	11, 22, 23
Ullock, Mary (Mrs. James Holmes)	35, 36, 37
University Park (Phoenix)	36
Van Deren, Mrs. James (Louisa J. Hawkins)	19
Varner, Walter "Bud"	52, 82
Venezuela (South America)	40, 49, 61, 65, 66, 82
Verde River (AZ)	10, 19, 67
Verde Valley (AZ)	1-117
Wager, Katie (Miss)	55
Walker, Ed	14
Wallace, Diana (Mrs. Timothy Oram)	77

Wallace, Mrs. George (Madeline Lee Stierwalt)	34, 63, 77, 78
Walnut Canyon (AZ)	59
Walsh, Margaret "Peggy" (Mrs. James W. Holmes)	71
Wetzler, Edna	48
Willard, Don	23
Williams (AZ)	57
Williams Air Force Base (AZ)	72
Windes, R. A. (Reverend)	25, 26
Wingfield, Francis	11
White Mountains (AZ)	57, 68
Whittier (CA)	66
Woods, Rube	30
Yuma (AZ)	88
Young, Herbert V.	18

*Note: Name and places in Appendix are not listed in the index.

The Masterpiece

Joyce MacLean

Arizona, land of glory,
Grips and holds the hearts of all--
Everything is filled with beauty,
Crevice, plain and mighty wall.

'Tis no marvel people love you
Land where friendship stands supreme,
The handwork of a mighty builder
Makes life seem a glorious dream.

Deserts some call drear and lonely
Are a wonder to behold--
All the colors of the rainbow
Mingle with the sands of gold.

Arizona with her splendor,
All her rich and fertile sod,
With her canyons, mountains, valleys-
Is the Masterpiece of God.

About the Author
Wyona Jaffe

Wyona was born in Phoenix while it was still a young town and watched it grow as she attended Murphy School and West Phoenix High School graduating in 1954. Her career in the school districts of Phoenix as Teacher's Aid, Clerk, Secretary and eventually, Secretary/Bookkeeper at Arizona State University Department of Public Safety set the stage for her eventual retirement to the Verde Valley where she had her roots.

Her grandmother, Jennie Lee Hawkins Holmes, was born in the Verde Valley and told Wyona stories about how she grew up in the Arizona Territory.

Her interest in the history of Arizona, set her on the path of writing *Jennie's Journal*. Her move to Lake Montezuma in 1986 gave her time and opportunity to finish the book, *Jennie's Journal: 1875 A True Story of a Verde Valley Pioneer*.

While living in the Verde Valley, Wyona became interested in helping the young people of Beaver Creek, so she joined the Beaver Creek Kiwanis in 2006 and served as secretary of the group for many years. She is a Charter Member of the Beaver Creek Baptist Church. as well a Charter Member and Board of Directors' Member of the Beaver Creek Preservation and

Historical Society. Her interest in the community prompted her to join the Lake Montezuma Women's Civic Club working on various committees and for the community as a whole. She spent three years serving on the Board of Directors for the Lake Montezuma/Rimrock Fire Department (now known as Copper Canyon Fire and Medical).

Wyona's intense love for the state of Arizona created in her a desire to paint the scenery she loves so much; especially the wildflowers. She eventually, also took up the hobby of photography and has developed slide shows teaching others how to identify the names of wildflowers of Arizona. She looks forward to releasing a layman's guidebook for wildflower identification. Look for: *Arizona Wildflower Logbook* packed with beautiful photographs of the Arizona wildflowers.

Contact Information
Author is available for speaking and books
May be contacted at
email: azwildflower137@gmail.com

Order books through:
Glorybound Publishing @
www.gloryboundpublishing.com
www.amazon.com

or directly from the author.

Made in the USA
Lexington, KY
27 October 2019